P9-CFS-502

ALSO BY LINDA GREENLAW

The Hungry Ocean
The Lobster Chronicles

ALL

FISHERMEN

ARE LIARS

ALL

FISHERMEN

ARE LIARS

True Tales from the Dry Dock Bar

LINDA GREENLAW

HYPERION NEW YORK

Library of Congress Cataloging-in-Publication Data

Greenlaw, Linda
  All fishermen are liars : true tales from the Dry Dock bar / Linda Greenlaw.
    p. cm.
  ISBN: 1-4013-0070-7
    1. Saltwater fishing—Anecdotes. 2. Fishers—Anecdotes. I. Title.

SH457.G63 2004
799.16—dc22

                                                    2004040609

FIRST EDITION

10 9 8 7 6 5 4 3 2 1

This book is dedicated to Aubrey and Addison, the next generation of fishermen.

CONTENTS

CONTENTS

Note to Readers

When I decided to write what has now become my third book, I could only hope that there might be someone who was interested in hearing more from me. I was full of apprehension and fear—that old, familiar feeling, the same combination that causes shortness of breath and a fluttering in the belly each time the lines are cast off the dock—that perhaps I had caught my last fish the trip before. I tried to approach this challenge just as I have everything in my life, with a balance of abundant enthusiasm and fear. With two memoirs under my belt at the age of forty-three, I knew I might need to live another twenty years to gather enough material for another book just about me. And the truth is, I am sick to death of Linda Greenlaw, and have been not so secretly yearning to tackle a work of fiction. A seagoing epic tale by Linda Greenlaw, novelist.

But, no. This was not to be. What caught my imagination was the idea of doing another nonfiction book, this one a collection of sea stories of the type I have spent so many hours swapping across bars up and down the Eastern Seaboard. Nonfiction sea stories? The more I thought about this oxymoron, the more excited I grew.

So, fiction will just have to wait. Instead, here is my book of absolutely true sea stories, collected one memorable night in one of my favorite watering holes, the Dry Dock bar (officially the Dry Dock Restaurant and Tavern) in Portland, Maine. (I've also included various extraneous lists and anecdotes; these I've called "Bar Snacks.") Fortunately, I do have an excellent memory and can recall quite accurately what transpired that evening. The Dry Dock is an actual establishment, and Alden is indeed a real person. All of the characters referred to within these pages are authentic and are referred to by their real names, and each and every instance and situation and conversation is neither fabricated nor exaggerated for dramatic effect or protection. There are no composites used. Every date and detail and description is accurate and completely well grounded in fact. Honest.

ALL

—

FISHERMEN

—

ARE LIARS

1

Getting
Under Way

I was a bit nervous about meeting Alden for lunch even though I realized this was ridiculous. But I wondered how Alden, after twenty-five years of being on the offering end of advice in our friendship, would react to listening to what had become a major concern of mine: his health. Twenty-seven years my senior, Alden considers himself wiser than me, and I suppose in most matters this is true. However, this truly tough, outspoken mentor of mine does not always use good judgment when it comes to his own well-being, and I had become worried to the point of being scared. Anyone in his right mind who had undergone heart surgery and understood the doctor's prognosis that Alden had received would be timid about getting out of bed in the morning, never mind climbing aboard a boat and heading offshore to haul lobster traps until well after dark. Today, I had vowed to myself, would be the time to broach the subject of Alden's retirement from fishing. This would not be easy.

Having spent most of my life fishing offshore, I tend to see the world through salt-rimmed glasses. My friend, far saltier than I, claims to have "pissed more saltwater than you have sailed over," and this might be true. Fishing is not what Alden does for a living; it is what he is. The fact that Alden had been diagnosed with congestive heart failure and had barely survived the installation of various pieces of hardware and a pacemaker/defibrillator was an indication to me that fishing might well be the death of Alden. Even lobstering can be brutal work, and Alden too frequently goes out alone. But suggesting to Alden that he give up fishing was like asking him to give up life. My best friend's entire identity and life are killing him, I thought as I drove to Portland; what a quandary.

Walter Alden Leeman Jr. has been my best friend since 1979. People always look at me strangely when I introduce Alden to them as "my best friend." They smile politely and shake his hand, but their eyes show thoughts of disbelief like, "You're kidding, right? This short, fat old man is your best friend?" I have been witnessing this reaction from others ever since the start of our friendship, and now feel compelled to explain what most folks regard as an unlikely pairing.

Readers weary of books in the inspirational mode can relax. Although I do often refer to Alden as a mentor, I am quick to qualify. I have received some of the worst advice (professional and personal) from my best friend, Alden Leeman. While his friendship has enriched my life, his influence hasn't all been for the good. Apparently, it never was intended to be all good, as is evident in the amount of pride Alden takes in claiming to have created "quite a monster."

In the realm of bad advice, Alden's has been the best. The first pearl of wisdom Alden gave me was the instruction not to bother paying back my student loan. In his opinion, no one paid the government back for college loans and I should not be a sucker. "Hell, if you wait 'em out, you'll receive amnesty like all of the others." The only things I received from the government were interest and penalties. Alden was at least consistent in his financial advice, urging me to treat American Express similarly. It cost me a small fortune to square with the IRS, and there's not a credit card company that will touch me. Even the Money Store and "Credit for Losers" laugh when I apply.

Alden's counsel for me in the personal-relations department has not been stellar. How many times have I endured the following unsolicited recommendation: "You have a lot to do in this lifetime, and you do not need a man dragging you down. You get too serious with some jerk and he'll be like an anchor around your neck. And never get married until you are just too old to do anything else."

In addition to receiving poor advice, I have learned most of my bad habits from my observations of, and association with, Alden. To his credit, Alden never set out to teach me to drink like a fish or swear like a pirate—those attributes just sort of rubbed off during our many years of friendship.

The many years began when, at the age of nineteen, I signed on as a crew member aboard Alden's swordfishing vessel. Commercial fishing was, at that time, a summer job to help pay my college tuition. I literally fished my way through school with Alden as my captain. Looking back twenty-four years, I am unsure whether my initial infatuation was with the captain or with the lifestyle of the blue-water fisherman. But I don't suppose it matters much now. The first eight years of my fishing career were in the employ of Alden, and he gave me my first shot at being a captain. I can say with confidence that Alden Leeman is one of the savviest fishermen (or boat people, in general) that I have met in all my time on, in, and around saltwater. I have learned more from my best friend than I have from everyone else from whom I've learned anything—and that's saying a lot, as I can learn something from anyone.

Fishing, gear, seamanship, navigation, boats, rigging—all very important aspects of my education, but nowhere near as interesting as the life lessons Alden has unknowingly shared. And nothing is more fun for me to talk about than what I would refer to as the "incidental education" bestowed upon me in my alliance with Alden. Perhaps one of the more poignant revelations that has come to me from our relationship is that there is quite a variety of bases on which to pin a friendship. The barometer for friendship covers a wide range. If asked to explain my friendship with Alden, I would answer with something like, "Alden has been a great mentor in my career, as well as a confidant in my personal affairs. Alden has always been there for me (yadda, yadda . . .). He has helped me out financially on many occasions, never asking a single question as to why I might need several thousand dollars at any given time." Alden, if asked the same question about me, would respond, "Linda is my best friend because she has bailed me out of jail more than once, and pulled me out of the ocean twice too." Alden has not learned a single thing from me, nor has he ever asked for my opinion or for my advice about anything. It's not that I haven't had any to offer, but, unlike Alden, I have never been one to push unsolicited into someone else's business. Today would be different.

One of the neatest lessons I have soaked up in the course of our friendship is always to recognize the special look in a man's eyes just before he punches another man's lights out. It is a very particular and definite look, and one that I have witnessed many times just prior to my friend getting the shit beaten out of him in a barroom. Alden is adamant about never having hit another man first, but I am usually around to remind him that he also has a knack for taunting the most innocent and gentle person into swinging a roundhouse to his nose. The word "goad" comes to mind when contemplating Alden's social graces.

In spite of his bad habits and shortcomings, Alden is the most amazing man I've ever encountered and has been my most loyal friend. I feel privileged to have been influenced, both negatively and positively, by our friendship—and I wonder how I could ever think of him in the past tense.

Today, damned close to the age of seventy, Alden has fortunately mellowed to a state that allows some people (in addition to me) actually to like him. Although this helped me feel relatively sure that we would not be tossed from the Dry Dock bar, where we had agreed to meet, I nervously hoped that Alden had matured enough to take to heart the advice I would soon be giving him. That our relationship had ripened was evident from the mature nature of the topics of our conversation while alone. In the company of others, we were as adolescent as ever, all talk being of boats and fishing.

As I entered the bar, I was disheartened to see it was crowded, so I anticipated more shoptalk than the pouring out of hearts. I wasn't surprised, just disappointed. Thanks to a combination of great location and great food, the Dry Dock is seldom quiet. Located on Portland's Commercial Street, the Dry Dock is a short walk downhill for merchants and bankers and lawyers whose places of business are in the Old Port section of Maine's largest city. To its east is a ferry terminal that accommodates boats servicing the islands of Casco Bay, and to its west are working docks. So, there is always an interesting mix of patrons. I poked my head around the door and saw that Alden had also just arrived. I first noticed that his hair, which he wears as short as possible without actually shaving his scalp, was totally white. When did that happen? I wondered. His face was as red as always and his eyes the same deep blue. I nearly made the mistake of mentioning his personal patriotic display of our flag's colors, but bit my tongue. I had a mission, and didn't want to get off focus. Alden would never forgive me if I were so foolish as to mention his failing health in front of anyone. So, I would have to be careful. It would be a chore to get Alden to share anything other than his many sea stories.

Almost everyone loves a sea story. And unless it's the deck of a boat, there's no better forum for sea stories than a barroom. The beauty of the barroom is the audience. A waterfront watering hole lends itself to top performances in that the storytellers must reach a broad audience. It's a challenge, really, and the most successful events begin one on one, two fishing buddies sharing a beer. There's a special knack the best storytellers have that draws an audience in, and a real pride they take in watching total strangers strain to listen while pretending to carry on their peripheral boredom. The greatest talent is exhibited by those who inspire uninvited participation from what was once the audience. No one is better at gathering a crowd than my friend Alden.

Our usual greeting of a warm bear hug assured me that he hadn't lost his tremendous strength, and the joy in his face indicated that he was in top form and ready to have a good time. He seemed to sense my intention to talk about something unfamiliar, and that this made me uneasy, and was at the top of his game in steering the conversation and all attention elsewhere. But one of the many lessons I have learned from Alden is persistence.

BAR SNACK

FREQUENTLY USED EXCUSES FOR NO FISH

1. The bait was rotten.
2. The weather was unfishable.
3. Inferior gear or tackle.
4. They weren't biting.
5. Incompetent crew.
6. Broken or outdated equipment or boat.
7. Wind from the east.
8. No fish around.
9. Spot fished out.
10. Too many sharks.

EXCUSE NEVER USED FOR NO FISH

1. I'm a lousy fisherman.

SEAMANSHIP

Unless the weather is awful enough to keep Portland's fishing fleet tied to the few remaining commercial wharfs, the lunchtime crowd at the Dry Dock is mostly the type that wears business casual. Well, it was just before Christmas, and the weather was bad enough to line the bar with some familiar fishing faces supported by necks braced in hooded sweatshirts—the men with neckties huddled in twos and fours at the many sturdy wooden tables forming the next band out from the core of the bar. Today there was a definite third ring, at the perimeter window seats and far corners, comprised of shoppers with bags at their feet, island dwellers waiting for the next ferry, and a table of four women who had the look of a luncheon bridge club. They appeared to be taking a break from a rigorous morning of cards for the best haddock sandwiches in town and glasses of wine.

"Sit at the bar?" Alden asked, nodding toward the only empty stools.

"No, let's wait for that table," I responded with a nod in the opposite direction. There was a young couple who seemed to be paying their bill.

"The bar would be more fun."

"We're not here for fun. We're here for lunch. And besides, look who's at the bar—George Pusey and Tommy Tucker. No way are we sitting near them." I took a step toward the table about to be vacated by the young couple and prayed that the two fishermen would not see us. They might possibly behave like humans in this atmosphere, but why take a chance? I considered the probability of sounding paranoid, and decided not to mention my theory that these two men had been following me for the past several years. I thought I had seen the last of them when I left swordfishing, and then they showed up on my island with a leaky old wooden lobster boat. They weren't any better at catching lobster than they had been with swordfish, so they resorted to becoming handymen. When the Island Boys repair and maintenance business went under, George and Tommy left the Island for Portland and found a couple of rusted slabs with which to attempt fishing again.

"G.P. and Double T, I'll be damned . . . I haven't seen them in a million years. We should say 'Hi' and buy them a drink," Alden suggested. Was his memory really that poor? I wondered. Turning to face my friend, I crossed my arms at my chest and stared into his eyes, hoping not to have to remind him of a previous encounter that had left him unconscious. Of course, that was in another bar on the other side of Commercial Street, one of the "three doors of hell," as the fishermen refer to the three raucous drinking establishments stumbling distance from the Dry Dock. I suspected that George and Tommy's presence on this side of the street might have been due to their having been banished from the rowdier spots. I couldn't remember a single time I had ever seen either of the pair leave a bar unescorted by bouncers or men in blue uniforms. I had a vision of blue flashing lights in our near future. A spark of recognition was followed by a broad smile as Alden had a change of heart about where we should sit. "Let's grab that table before someone else gets it." So, we took seats at a newly vacated table next to the ladies' bridge group.

As I hung my jacket on the back of my chair and sat down, I couldn't help but notice that Alden looked tired. I was certain that he must be consumed by concern for his health and might be relieved to have a candid conversation with me, sharing worries and perhaps finding some consolation in confiding his deepest thoughts and fears. Alden surveyed the room like a cowboy looking for a gunfight and finally sat with his back against the wall. I knew Alden well enough to realize he would never initiate dialogue on a subject he would generally regard as "soft" or "girl talk." Real men don't discuss their health problems in a barroom. Over a drink with a buddy, real men speak only of snow tires and baseball and fishing. I would have to take the lead and bring up a tough subject for the benefit of both of us. I took a deep breath and wondered why this was so difficult. Why couldn't I just ask if he was scared? Why couldn't I simply tell him that he had to retire to prolong his life? Just as I was steeling myself to jump in, Alden spoke.

"Whatever happened to Alan? I really liked him." Alden was inquiring about the only male friend of mine he had ever approved of, a man with whom I hadn't spoken in years. So much for a deep, personal, emotional talk between old friends, I thought. Before I could answer with the usual "Things just didn't work out," a waitress was inquiring about beverages. I ordered a glass of Chardonnay and waited for Alden to think about what he might like to drink. I knew that he would eventually order a rum and Coke, but he did not know this. He never did. He would think, and look over at the bottles lining the shelves above the bar, and remark on the beautiful stainless-steel swordfish sculpture above them. Then he would think some more while the waitress patiently waited for him to order the rum and Coke. Alden was certainly "clever like a fox" with his mention of an ex-guyfriend. He had really thrown me off course, and I sensed that it had been intentional. While he thought and the waitress waited, I had time to relive my entire relationship with Alan, the nicest man with the worst luck.

I first met Alan, with whom I enjoyed a part-time relationship (part-time because we both spent most of our calendar years aboard fishing boats), over the airwaves of the single-side-band (SSB) radio. A very distant voice with a slight southern accent was quite persistently and unsuccessfully trying to "raise" the captain of the swordfishing vessel *Sealion VIII*. Over and over as I steamed the *Hannah Boden* west along the temperature break into which 40 miles of my longlining gear would soon unfurl, I heard a voice calling, "*Sealion Eight, Sealion Eight,* the *Miss Gertrude.* Whiskey, tango, alpha, two, zero, niner, four. Pick me up, Larry?"

I knew the *Miss Gertrude* as a dragger, or stern trawler, whose homeport was Newport, Rhode Island, and who had recently begun to fish out of Portland, Maine. The *Miss Gertrude* was currently rigged for "groundfishing," which means towing a net across the ocean floor for flounder, monkfish, cod, haddock, hake, cusk, redfish, pollock, and the like. At this time, the *Miss Gertrude* was probably working a piece of bottom either in the Gulf of Maine or on the northern edge of George's Bank. The *Sealion VIII* was a swordfish longline vessel owned and operated by my fishing buddy Larry Thompson, called L.T. I assumed that L.T. was not responding to the radio because he did not hear the many calls; he was fishing less than 100 miles from me, east of the Grand Banks of Newfoundland. When I just could not bear one more unanswered call, I grabbed the microphone of the *Hannah Boden*'s SSB radio and hailed L.T. myself. The answer was prompt and gruff, exactly the demeanor I expected from L.T. given that I was contacting him during the most stressful time of day. Late afternoon into early evening finds the captains of swordfishing vessels jockeying for position and strategizing about how to fine-tune, or at least improve, the night's setting of the hooks.

I explained to Larry that the captain of the *Miss Gertrude* had been calling him at five-minute intervals for over an hour. "Well, obviously I can't hear him. Linda, would you relay that to him? His name is Alan." And I did relay this message to Alan, who was grateful to finally get an answer from someone, even if it was not the captain he intended to speak to. By the end of "our" conversation, in which I served as the go-between, repeating transmissions back and forth for both men, I realized that Alan was probably relieved to have me as a buffer to cushion the news that he was so compelled to deliver, namely that he (Alan) had wrecked his (Larry's) Harley-Davidson.

L.T. did not seem overwrought about the bike, which may

have been a reflection of the time of day. Larry's real concern, after learning that Alan had not been injured, was what my plan of attack was to be for tonight's set—my readings of the water temperature, position, current, and other information pertinent to successful fishing. After patiently listening to the two of us compare notes, thoughts, theories, strategies, and weather reports, Alan politely interjected that he wanted to assure L.T. that the crumpled bike would be repaired upon the *Sealion VIII*'s return to the dock. (Which seemed quite likely, as the errant Evel Knievel came across as sincere, was calling from the dock, and had at least two weeks before Larry would call it a trip.) Wow, what misfortune, I thought, to smash up a borrowed Harley-Davidson. So, as an incidental third party to radio transmissions from an unlucky man unfortunate enough to lose control of a bike belonging to someone else is, in retrospect, where my entry into the world of Alan should have ended. But of course it did not.

For the remainder of that trip I relayed progress reports of the motorcycle's repairs from the *Miss Gertrude*, who remained tied to the wharf, to the still-at-sea *Sealion VIII*. Estimates were given, the bike was delivered to a Hog mechanic, the bike was disassembled, parts were ordered, parts were not delivered, the wrong parts were delivered, the wrong parts were returned, the correct parts arrived, the correct parts were ignored by the mechanic for several frustrating days, and finally the motorcycle was whole again. It seemed, I thought, the most hoodooed series of events. The bike's being up and running was my final relay to L.T., after which Alan thanked me profusely and promised to buy me lunch should we ever bump into each other on a dock somewhere.

• • •

The next time I was in Portland, I happened to find Alan on the dock beside which his boat, the *Miss Gertrude,* was secured. The stocky redhead invited me to go for a ride on the back of his newly purchased Yamaha. Why I agreed to do so is beyond me, as the only concrete things I knew about the man were that he caught fish for a living and had crashed a friend's bike not long ago, neither of which was a reason for joining him in any venue, much less over the rear axle of a quick new motorcycle. The short ride was smoother and more pleasant than the termination of the relationship that formed in its dust.

Bad things just kept happening to Alan. Bad things turned to terrible things, and when I verbalized my amazement at the quantity and degree of misfortune that had befallen him since I had made his acquaintance, Alan assured me that the situation was not new. In fact, he claimed, bad luck had been plaguing him for some time in the form of mechanical problems, high prices when he had no fish, low prices when he had a boatload, and breaches of agreements, broken promises, and basic shortcomings of integrity and honor in literally everybody with whom Alan conducted business. I had never met anyone with such a propensity for being cheated, ripped off, and lied to. But the most remarkable stretch of strange occurrences that I either witnessed firsthand or got straight from the horse's mouth all involved Alan's crew members, some of whom may make reference to the horse's other end with regards to their once captain.

I was only a bit surprised to learn that one of Alan's "transit guys" (a fisherman who fills in for an occasional trip) had written himself a check or two from the *Miss Gertrude*'s checkbook, but not as horrified as someone in any other industry might feel upon hearing about this kind of offense. In the world of fishing, it often seems that anything goes. Alan chose to not press charges, happy to see the end of the loser transit man. I was disturbed, however, when one of his crew members sucker-punched Alan in the face, knocking him from his feet. Totally unprovoked (oh, except for a perceived short paycheck), the man had slugged his captain and walked away, never to be seen again. And I was mortified, and a bit grossed out, to hear about the lengths to which another crew member had gone to make a statement: He shit in Alan's briefcase. That's right—a disgruntled (so to speak) employee relieved himself on top of the checkbook inside Alan's briefcase, closed the cover of the case, and put it in its proper place on the chart table as a nice surprise for the captain. Then Alan's luck turned from the bizarre and hostile to the profoundly sad.

A young, bright, and handsome deckhand had been fishing aboard the *Miss Gertrude* for several trips to earn college money when his leg came within a small strip of skin from being totally severed from his body in an accident that naturally had quite an impact on Alan. The injured man was airlifted from the boat's deck and rushed to the hospital, where the initial prognosis was that the leg would be lost. I imagined it had to have been the longest night of Alan's life—surely, I thought, this had to be the grand finale of the hostile cloud that hovered over the dispirited captain of the *Miss Gertrude*. And it seemed for a relative instant to be so.

The injured deckhand underwent several surgeries. The leg

was miraculously saved, and to the best of my knowledge is in decent working order. But the whole traumatic episode took its toll on Alan.

Alan was not a lot of fun to be around anymore. Our relationship wore thin. Alan lost what remained of his enthusiasm for the *Miss Gertrude.* He lost what bit of pleasure he still felt for an industry that once thrilled him. He lost that last shred of optimism that things could not stay bad forever. He lost the twinkle in his green eyes and the chuckle in his voice. He lost his courage to leave the dock, and hired a captain to run his beloved *Miss Gertrude.* Initially, my tendency was to encourage Alan to relinquish the reins of his boat to another captain. I had fished aboard the *Miss Gertrude* for a few trips and had not considered the never-ending mishaps anything more than coincidental. But in light of all the bad luck that had come Alan's way, I had begun to regard the boat as possessed, and thought that Alan, who was nearing the bitter end of his emotional and financial rope, might benefit, in both categories, from some distance.

Mechanical problems, poor fishing, crooked cooks hightailing it with the "grub money" . . . the saga continued. Now Alan's situation went from awful to desperate. He dragged his feet, but begrudgingly acquiesced to the reality that he would have to repossess the captain's chair in order to relieve some of his financial woes. Paying his debts and a salary wasn't working. The announcement that he would un-retire was painstaking and dramatic, but it did seem that he didn't have much of a choice. And to his credit, Alan was not a quitter—this was one of the reasons Alden liked him. When I learned of Alan's decision, I knew how difficult it would be for him to return to a life he had grown to hate with intensity, but understood that the dreaded move was his last stab at salvaging a shred of pride.

As it turned out, Alan never got the opportunity to fish himself out of Chapter 11. While waiting for the hired captain to return the boat to the dock, Alan received a phone call from the Coast Guard. The *Miss Gertrude* had capsized in bad weather and had sunk offshore.

My thoughts at the time included the sense that the only positive thing resulting from this tragedy, although I realize it was a stretch, was that Alan was now free of the evil boat. This was an opportunity for my downtrodden friend to start afresh, begin a new career perhaps. Things would improve—they couldn't get any worse, I thought. I was unsuccessful in attempts to force Alan to look on the bright side. Now the man with the lost spirit, hope, sense of humor, twinkle, chuckle, and optimism had also lost his identity. To put it quite simply, Alan quickly became the most negative son of a bitch on the planet. Then, although dear friends tried to discourage him from doing so, Alan borrowed enough money to add to the insurance settlement and a small inheritance to buy *two* boats in order to replace what was missing in his life. Not just any two boats—two of the neediest vessels afloat. I traveled to Florida to take a peek at the first purchase and didn't dare climb aboard for fear of falling through the rusted deck plates. She was a mess. She was a disaster, and had to be towed the length of the Eastern Seaboard to a shipyard for a total reconstruction.

Alan, a very clever fixer and fabricator, was certainly capable all by himself of every bit of overhauling and refitting necessary to get both boats up and running, given enough time. But the amount of work needed on the first vessel was too extensive for one man to handle quickly, so Alan started hiring. Somewhat limited by availability, he brought on a couple of felons involved in a work-release program to help with some of the dirtier, more manual, less skilled tasks. After a few hours spent cleaning sludge from the insides of fuel tanks (requiring the men to *be* inside the tanks), even the convicts found the chore too arduous and disgusting, and opted to return to jail cells rather than hang with the new boss. The boss became discouraged with the project, but having mortgaged himself into a corner, had nothing to do but sweat and slave his way out of it. Every swing of the chipping hammer fed the downward spiral of Alan's entire being. I have to admit that by this time I was so weary of constant bad news and negativism that I terminated, as gently as I could, the remains of our relationship/friendship. I had no regrets about doing so, and only thought of Alan when Alden brought him up.

Alden had ordered the rum and Coke and sat anticipating an answer to his question of what had become of Alan. I didn't find it strange that he should ask about Alan after so much time had elapsed, as the Dry Dock was Alan's favorite unwinding spot and George and Tommy were two of his closest friends. (As an aside, I never thought George and Tommy were good influences in Alan's life. Alan was a super-educated, nice, hardworking gentleman. George and Tommy are, well, not.) Rather than go into the long-winded version of the eclipsed relationship, I gave Alden the reply that I had rehearsed with so many other inquiries. "Oh, things just didn't work out. Distance was a problem. Alan is a Rhode Islander, and I'm a Mainer. We couldn't afford the phone bills."

Alden, who has always been skeptical of women and relationships that last longer than fifteen minutes, chuckled. "Rhode Island to Maine . . . what's that? A couple hundred miles? Sounds perfect to me. Does he have a sister?" This I chose to ignore and got very interested in the menu. Neither Alden nor I had to wonder about or discuss the fact that fishermen often have trouble maintaining relationships, and I suppose it's true of anyone who chooses to go to sea for extended periods. Absence does not always make the heart grow fonder. And true love of saltwater often supersedes that of the flesh.

I knew from past experience that deciding on and ordering lunch would be a major dilemma for my friend, and the sooner he started staring at the choices, the better the chance he'd actually order before dinnertime. My prompting failed. Alden had become infatuated with the group of women at the table behind me and I held my breath as I waited for him to make some embarrassing remark a little too loudly. Alden does not have a mean streak, but he does have poor hearing, probably caused by so many years with diesel engines. This coupled with the fact that Alden never thinks before speaking has resulted in my wanting to crawl under the table on several occasions. For example: Sitting beside Alden in a movie theater, just as the lights dimmed before the show began, when everyone got very quiet, Alden asked, "Did you see that woman's teeth?" And of course I had. It would have been impossible to miss them. An elbow to his ribs didn't stop him, and he added, "I'll bet she could eat an apple through a picket fence." I shrank down in my seat and covered both ears

with my hands to muffle his final, "She could be Mister Ed's cousin."

I have tried to explain to Alden that he needs to turn the volume down when verbalizing his observations of others, but he always seems hurt and replies with, "Wait until you get to be my age." Now, Alden was clearly entertained by what he was gawking at and even started to laugh. Because I was across the table from him, I couldn't reach him with an elbow, so I began my hardest, dirtiest looks, hoping to distract him from whatever rude thought he was surely about to blurt out. His focus remained on the group of women, and he was oblivious to every rotten and disgust-filled facial expression I could conjure up to silence him. If it hadn't been for the table and me separating them, one would have thought Alden a part of the group at the next table. He was engrossed in the happenings at the supposed bridge gathering. He was now laughing so hard his eyes watered. As he wiped a tear from his cheek with the back of a weathered hand, he said, "They sound like humpback whales in mating season!"

Fortunately, I knew the scene well from so many Thursday-afternoon regroupings in my mother's living room. I didn't need to turn around and look at the women to know that they had all pulled date books and personal organizers from oversize handbags and were now at the stage of figuring out when they would have the next game and lunch. I could hear them all explaining their various obligations and the commitments keeping them from this day or that time. Why, there were art galleries and wine tastings and grandchildren's school plays . . . I was always amazed that the next game ever actually got scheduled. Alden slapped a knee and laughed even harder as the women maintained four separate and

distinct narratives of social obligations. Thank goodness they were oblivious to the man they were entertaining. Sensing that the waitress was reaching the end of her patience, I ordered a crabmeat sandwich for myself and fried clams for Alden. The door to the kitchen closed behind our waitress before Alden could interrogate her about when and where the clams had been dug. No matter; Alden shrugged and focused again on the incessant chatter at the adjacent table. Slowly the sound of an approaching train silenced the women; indeed, the entire bar and restaurant fell quiet.

There was no train. The rumble was that of heavy wind on the windows and brick walls; every ear in the place twitched, and bodies shivered. All eyes turned and looked out at the cold street, watching wispy snow clouds tumble low to the ground and disappear over the water in Portland Harbor. It was a typical December day on the waterfront. "Storm warnings up for tonight and tomorrow," Alden said, referring to the marine weather forecast. I was silently thankful to be here with my best friend rather than offshore. And, oddly enough, I felt a slight twinge of guilt for not being at sea. I wondered out loud how many boats were out, how many captains had decided to remain at sea rather than beat and pound into the northwest gale to secure to a dock. "Those who bet against the weatherman's accuracy today made a poor decision," was Alden's answer, reminding me of a time when I had done the same. I was certain that I had never shared the experience with Alden, and feeling lucky to be alive to tell the story, launched into it as soon as the waitress returned with some bread and butter. A sea story was a more comfortable topic than Alden's poor health. Perhaps telling a story would help me to ease into something serious.

• • •

It was March 1993 when the marine radio announced that "the storm of the century" was bearing down on us, but the announcement came too late for me to run. I was engaged in the offshore lobster fishery with the *Hannah Boden* at the time. Offshore lobstering is similar to the inshore fishery only in method; baited traps are fished. Bigger boats with more crew members work weeklong trips in and around the "canyons," where the continental shelf drops off to deep water, as opposed to working the shoal water around the shore where I presently fish a 35-footer with my father. The weather was perfect for shifting gear (moving traps from one area to another): flat-calm and clear. And the forecast held nothing to make me nervous about loading the *Hannah Boden* to her maximum capacity. The crew and I had been hoping to wait to move the 1,400 lobster traps until May, when we would have been happy to take them ashore and rig the boat for our preferred vocation—longlining swordfish. The traps that we had been fishing since December, in and around the canyons just west of the Hague Line, hadn't produced much in the past two trips, resulting in the boss's insistence that we shift the gear southwest, to the edge of the continental shelf between the Baltimore Canyon and Cape Hatteras.

"If the weather stays this pretty, we'll be able to shift everything in three trips." I tried to sound optimistic and happy about the amount of work we had ahead of us, knowing, as did every one of my six-man crew, that the next ten days would be ones during which no money would be made. The weeks following the shift would be questionable in the way of paychecks too, as the months of April and May had always been tough ones no matter whether I was fishing for swordfish, halibut, groundfish, or lobster. Until the full moon in June, we would be putting in time and grinding out expenses with just a few lobsters to show for it, all in anticipation of our first swordfish trip, which we hoped would give us the income we desperately needed.

We hauled, stacked, and secured the last of a dozen forty-pot trawls (forty traps secured to one line) to be transported on this trip, and I headed the *Hannah Boden* southwest for what should have been a thirty-six-hour steam. The *Hannah Boden* was built with lobster fishing in mind. She is 100 feet in length and has enormous deck space to handle large loads of traps. If the weather had not been quite so nice, and the forecast so great, I would never have asked the men to stack the gear high enough to allow nearly five hundred traps in one jaunt. The fishing had become so poor that it made sense to get the traps to greener pastures as quickly as possible. "Not even five hundred pounds," came the lobster tally delivered to me with a sandwich by D.J., a true lobster fisherman and the only member of the crew not holding his breath waiting for sword season.

"That's why we're going for a ride," I replied. "Couldn't ask for better weather." Twenty-four hours later, I couldn't have imagined worse weather or a more terrifying situation.

We were steaming along just below Hudson Canyon, the *Hannah Boden* looking more like a container ship than a fishing vessel now with her full load of traps, when something drew my attention from the book in my lap. I listened, and realized that all of the conversations on both VHF and SSB radios were about a storm that until right then I had known nothing about. Interested, I left my perch in the wheelhouse chair, tossed *A Confederacy of Dunces* onto the chart table, and turned up the volume of the SSB radio that I had managed to tune out while laughing my way through my all-time favorite book. Within thirty minutes of bits and pieces of many transmissions, I gathered that every vessel off the Eastern Seaboard was heading for the barn, running from what sounded like a whopper of an ocean storm. Now I was concerned and went about the business of amassing all of the weather information available to me aboard the *Hannah Boden*, and there was plenty of information available.

The computer-generated voices of the weather services coming from both radios, the fax machine printouts of surface analyses and twenty-four-hour prognosis maps, the satellite receiver's weather-tracking system, and all ship reports concurred: We were bound to get our asses kicked unless we joined the rest of the fleet and headed to the safety of the nearest port. "I might be able to make Cape May, or Barnegat Inlet might be better. But then I'd have farther to come after the storm passes." I was thinking out loud and getting ready to curse Mother Nature for inconveniencing me. "Friggin' storm couldn't possibly wait until this load of gear was off the deck."

Just as I was figuring our range and bearing from the nearest dock, and preparing to abandon my course to the fishing grounds, I heard a familiar voice on the radio. Everyone knows him as "Steve the Greek." Steve, whose last name has five syllables, is as tenacious a fisherman as I have ever known, and he was making it clear that he was not about to let a little weather push him off his "hot spot" where he was "bailing" the fish aboard. Just two canyons up the edge from my position, Steve and his crew on the *Panther* were busy cable fishing, catching groundfish with gear consisting of hooks clipped onto a small-diameter wire that lies on the bottom of the ocean until hauled back aboard. The *Pan-*

ther was not nearly as large and seaworthy as the *Hannah Boden,* although he often put her through some rigorous paces.

I began calculating again. I thought out loud, "Even if the storm does exactly what the weather gurus say, I should have time to reach my destination and set this gear out before the weather's upon us. Then who cares how hard it blows? We've ridden out worse. Besides, if we go in, I stand the chance of losing part or all of the crew in a barroom. The weather people are always so dramatic. Hype a low-pressure area, and suddenly there's big news." And with that sort of reasoning, I decided to remain on course and finish shifting this first load of traps.

That evening it was evident that the weather people had indeed been mistaken in their predictions concerning the storm's speed and intensity. It had traveled faster, and contained winds of much greater velocity, than anyone had anticipated. By the time I realized the severity of the system that was quickly bearing down on the *Hannah Boden,* I also realized the severity of my decision to remain at sea in spite of all warnings. The prudent thing to do at this point would have been to set out the mountain of gear that, although tied securely to the vessel, was extra weight above the boat's waterline and thus would dramatically decrease her stability. Problem? The wind had come up so fast, and the sea was now so steep, that I thought it would be dangerous to send the crew onto the deck for the setting-out process. There were no more poor decisions to make. All I could do now was ride out the storm and hope it passed quickly. I had made the proverbial bed, now seven of us had to lie in it.

The center of the low was southwest of my position, and the conditions were just less than miserable. The autopilot was doing a fine job of keeping the *Hannah Boden'*s bow up into the wind and we were comfortably climbing green foothills, sliding down the backsides, and climbing the next when something hit our port side so hard I was nearly knocked from my feet. Initially I was tempted to glance out the port-side windows for the ship that had run us down, or off the stern for the rock I had struck, as the sound and impact of the crash could have been caused by nothing less. But I had encountered rogue waves before, or a "queer sea," as the old-timers referred to the single wave that is so much bigger, and often attacks from a different direction than the others.

A queer sea marches to a different drummer, and I watched this one step away to starboard unscarred by its contact with the 100-foot steel vessel. We hadn't even made the slightest dent in the rogue that had left us in quite a state of danger. The jarring of the boat by the sea seemed to have knocked the hull out from under the stack of traps, which had now come to rest left of center, leaving us with a pronounced port list. Seamanship 101: Keep the boat on an even keel. Now we had weight up high *and* off center.

The *Hannah Boden* rolled deeply to port and hesitated for what seemed an eternity before returning to a position as upright as she could muster with the shifted load. Ivan was the first man to the wheelhouse from below. "Are you all right up here?" he asked. I was nervous at best, and snapped the autopilot off. Steering the boat by hand, I assured Ivan that I was fine and asked whether all was in one piece below. "Jesus! That felt like an explosion. Bounced me out of my rack, but no damage," he replied. Following a brief discussion of how to counter the list, Ivan, who had been serving as the boat's engineer for several months, raced down two flights to the engine room where he got busy transferring fuel to the available tank space on the high side of the boat. Moving fuel to the starboard side would offset the weight of the traps that had shifted to port. After the *Hannah Boden* took a couple more breathtaking dips to port, Ivan emerged with the report that he had done all he could. We had been away from the dock for only three days. Since we were at nearly full fuel capacity, there wasn't much room in the starboard tanks to transfer fuel to. The aft fish hold was currently being used as a storage area, and the gear and supplies in that compartment could have been shifted around to help alleviate the list if it had not been for the fact that the only access to the hold was buried under the mountain of traps. I had certainly managed to put us in a tight spot.

We seemed to be holding our own. I stayed at the wheel, steering to keep the wind and sea just off the bow to port. Ivan went below to "hang on," urging me to yell if I needed him to spell me at the helm. "In the meantime, I sure hope this weather doesn't get any worse," he said. I always enjoyed fishing with Ivan, but never appreciated him quite so much as I did right then. I knew that Ivan could be depended upon in any circumstance, which gave me peace of mind in the present situation. I also knew that I would not ask Ivan or anyone else to run the boat in bad weather and listing to port, as it is ultimately the captain who is responsible for the safety of the vessel and crew.

Continuing to quarter the boat into the waves, like a surfer lying on his board and paddling seaward, I adjusted the throttle up and down a couple of hundred rpms in an attempt to keep the ride as comfortable as I could. There is a fine line between enough speed through the water to maintain steerage and too much speed, which can result in possibly losing the wheelhouse windows or wiping out the antennas. To say I was paying attention would be an understatement. Playing the throttle would become more difficult, I knew, as darkness won over the light of day.

Once totally in the dark, I would have to feel rather than see what should be done with wheel and throttle, a nerve-racking exercise at best.

At dusk, two ships appeared on the horizon, huge super-tankers making their way to some port to off-load millions of gallons of oil. The ships appeared and vanished, appeared and vanished, with each rise and fall of the *Hannah Boden* from crest to trough, crest to trough like a bobbing jack-in-the-box. The wind was a steady 50 knots, with "occasional higher gusts."

Whenever I am recounting sea stories involving extreme weather to folks who prefer to remain landlocked, someone invariably asks, "How high were the seas?" Or, "What's the biggest wave you have ever seen?" My reply is something like, "Fishermen speak of weather in terms of wind velocity. I have no way to measure individual waves. You're up, you're down . . . how many feet? I know the difference between thirty knots of wind and fifty knots of wind. But the difference between a thirty-foot sea and a fifty-foot sea? I suspect it's a difference between 'this sucks' and 'this REALLY sucks.'" At this point in this story, it just sucked.

At the edge of darkness, the two tankers had drawn to a distance of 2 miles from my position, which was nearly static, as we were making less than .5 knots over ground. I heard one of the captains hail the other on VHF channel 16, and switched my radio to channel 10 along with them to listen to their opinions on the weather. What I learned did little to ease my mind. They had been ordered by the captain of the port to which they were heading to remain offshore until the weather eased, as the port's anchorage areas had become what one of the voices referred to as a "cluster fuck" of ships and boats ducking the elements, some of the ships already dragging anchors in weather that promised to get worse before the improvement tentatively scheduled for the following morning. So, it seemed I would have company for the night, as the two captains agreed to hang out until further notice. Just as I was about to pick up the microphone to make them aware of my presence and limited mobility, their attention and conversation shifted to "the idiots aboard that tiny fishing boat to the southwest." Not wanting to identify myself as the captain of the idiots, I waited and listened.

By 8:00 P.M. there had been a marked change in the weather. The wind had increased and with it the seas had finally graduated to "this REALLY sucks." One moment I was confident that I had the *Hannah Boden* under my authority, and the next I found my-self in that all-too-familiar tug-of-war with Mother Nature for control of the vessel. There was a brief sigh of relief in the trough of two mountainous seas; a feeling of being in the lee, protected from the screeching wind. A split second later, that sigh was re-placed by clenching of teeth and holding of breath as the boat teetered on a peak that pushed upward and momentarily grabbed the reins, then awkwardly relinquished them as the vessel wal-lowed unsurely down into the next trough. I became aware of my pulse as it fluctuated up and down with the boat, feeling a slight throbbing in my fingertips as I squeezed the wheel. There were moments of wondering, Who's driving?, brief interruptions that pierced the sheer concentration necessary to maintain any sense of perceived control.

At the very top of the largest of seas and at maximum expo-sure, the ferocity of the storm was heard more than it was felt as the wind found many pitches. The breeze whistled shrilly as it sought out the smallest openings in the boat. Stay wires hummed and vibrated as the wind T-boned itself around them, finally drumming against the wheelhouse windows that detoured each gust around the house and aft. What followed was a disconcerting sucking sound and a moment of terrifying silence. A falling feeling in the stomach obliterated anything auditory. Each descent from a crest was silent, and we instinctively spent it with bent knees, ready to absorb the impact of the fetching up at the bottom of the next trough. As we hit, my knees buckled each time, then straightened as my ears opened back up to a loud bang followed by a shudder and the applause of heavy spray. Then all would play again. After each cycle of up and down, I had the tendency to grip the wheel tighter to keep my feet squarely on the deck and fight the launching of my body up the next sea ahead of the boat. Over and over, top to bottom, working, working, working . . . After what seemed like hours, every muscle in my body was twitching and my ears were ringing to the rhythm of Edgar Allan Poe's "tintinnabulation of the bells, bells, bells, bells, bells, bells, bells."

The lines securing the load of traps to the deck and to each other had been loosened by the constant pitching of the boat, allowing the entire stack to wobble fore and aft, motion I found most disconcerting. A seamanship and stability nightmare: Now the excessive weight was not only too high and off center but it was also moving. The boat moved under the traps like a hand under a stack of fine china, teetering, threatening to crash, and then finding temporary balance. The more the stack of traps moved, the more the lines stretched and loosened, allowing the stack even more freedom of mobility. The weather was absolutely the worst I had ever encountered, and the motion of the gear was downright dangerous. But what could I do? I could send a man out to cut the lines, allowing the traps to jettison themselves. Too dangerous for the man, I decided. Eventually, if the lines continued to slacken, some of the traps would tumble overboard with no help from anyone but Mother Nature, and there would be nothing I could do to prevent that from happening except hope that it wouldn't, which was what I did. As nice as it would be to relieve some of the danger by losing traps by either method, that would improve neither the weather nor our financial woes.

The ship captains were back on the radio and once again comparing notes on wind velocity and their proximity to the little boat they were now having trouble finding in the sea return on their radar screens. My radar was still showing both ships at a distance of just better than 1 nautical mile from me. They were concerned because they could no longer distinguish my little steel-hulled fishing boat from the waves cluttering the centers of their radar screens, and worried that because of this, they might inadvertently get too close to me, especially if the conditions deteriorated and further hindered their maneuverability. Seeing as the captains had not referred to us as the "idiots" during this last exchange, I thought it wise to let them know that I was paying attention, and that we were all maintaining what I considered a safe distance, but that I was already extremely limited in maneuverability. (I was quite happy to have the ships this close. Just in case.)

Without sharing the embarrassing details of my less-than-optimum stability due to the traps now in perpetual motion, I had a pleasant, businesslike conversation with one of the captains, who was happy to inform me that the wind had increased to a brisk 70 knots. He spared me the agony of explanation by not asking the obvious, "What the hell are you doing out here?" He asked only that I keep an eye on the radar and let them know if the distance between us was closing. I agreed, and asked only one favor of him: "When and if the wind cranks up to one hundred knots, please do not bother telling me." I couldn't hang the mike up fast enough. I needed both hands on the wheel to keep myself upright.

The hours between midnight and daylight were the longest of my life. I felt as though we were engaged in an epic battle: The belt holder, Mother Nature, was throwing us around the ring like an outclassed, underweight underdog. Each time we were knocked down, we struggled back to our feet, only to get whacked again. The boisterous crowd of seas surrounding the arena urged us to stay down for the count, but we staggered and covered up and prayed for the bell. I knew the wind was blowing much harder than at the time of the last report and so wasn't surprised when one of the captains announced on the radio, "You said not to bother telling you the current wind speed, so I won't." Now the *Hannah Boden*'s hull and rigging were producing sounds I had never heard before. The creaks, groans, and moans were all the result of stress, and were causing the same in me. I groaned and moaned right along with her. The visual manifestation of the sound effects was on the crew members' faces as they appeared one at a time beside me at the wheel, under the guise of checking on me. Each of them seemed relieved to have the offer of taking the wheel for a while gratefully declined. Only Ivan lingered before heading back below to struggle along with the rest of his shipmates in their unsuccessful attempts to remain in their bunks, which kept falling out from under them and rising up again to meet them. Like beginning divers making repeated belly flops, the men kept finding themselves slammed facedown. Now Ivan stood near me, facing aft. With each lurch of the boat and shifting of the traps, Ivan winced. His eyes narrowed, his shoulders came up, shortening his neck, and he drew a quick breath through closed teeth. I could tell that Ivan was bracing himself for the lines finally to part and the traps to fly around and overboard. "What will we do if the lines part, Ma?" he asked.

"Wave good-bye to five hundred traps."

"Good riddance, I'd say." And with that, Ivan left to check the engine room and try to wedge himself into his bunk or at the galley table to endure the next thirty minutes until he would make the rounds again.

I steered the *Hannah Boden,* holding the wheel with both hands to prevent myself from being tossed around the bridge like Raggedy Ann on a possessed trampoline. And all the long while, I tried to convince myself that the worst was surely over, and be thankful that it was dark. If I had been able to see the weather, I thought I might possibly panic. I made a game of guessing when and where the lights of the tankers would pop out of the darkness, and even hummed, "Round and round the mulberry bush." I was miserable. I was exhausted. I questioned my career choice. I questioned my sanity. I promised myself that this would be my last trip, a vow I had broken several times in the past. Up we went. Up, up, up . . . I waited for the crest to push us backward, but we kept going up. I pushed the throttle ahead slightly as the climb felt steeper than before. Ahhh, there it was. Finally the crest balanced the boat as if on the tip of a finger, and for a fraction of a second, the world was still. The silence was broken by Steve the Greek's announcement to the world over the SSB radio, "This fuckin' sucks."

I pulled the throttle back. The bow fell sharply and the boat followed in a dive. Every loose thing in the wheelhouse was now hanging in midair. Parallel rulers, dividers, and binoculars defied gravity. As the dive slowed slightly, the suspended articles caught up with the hull and landed like hailstones around me. A book fell out of the sky like a dead bird, hitting me on the back of my neck. "Ouch!" I looked to see what had hit me and saw that it was *A Confederacy of Dunces.* How appropriate, I thought, and wondered if just two, Steve and I, constituted a confederacy. The angle of descent decreased as the mountainous sea crept away, allowing our stern to drop a bit. The dive became a free fall. I waited for the impact and was not disappointed. Crash! I thought the *Hannah Boden* had come unglued. We rolled deeply to port, buried the port outrigger, and lay there. I pushed the throttle to full ahead and wondered if she would get back on her feet before the next wave attempted to roll us over.

It was painful. Every joint creaked and every muscle trembled. The *Hannah Boden,* sweating and shaking, pulled herself from the ocean's grasp and back into the upright world, which was just beginning to distinguish itself with a crease of light to the east. Yes, the streak of light was horizontal. I was not aware of Ivan's entrance, but there he was, holding on and shaking his head. He laughed, and I have always wondered what he found amusing. Well, that was the worst of it. As quickly as the sun came up, the wind dropped out. The seas went from steep, jagged faces to smooth, rolling swells that gently kissed good-bye the twelve hours of sheer hell we had endured.

"And we never lost a single trap," I added as I concluded my worst-storm story just as our lunch was set before us. Good seamanship may have been the difference between life and death in the midst of that storm, and I had learned most of what I know of seamanship from Alden, who taught me that good seamanship is 50 percent common sense and 50 percent experience. Common sense told me that I needed to have a frank talk with Alden regarding his insistence on continuing to work. Experience told me that the time was not quite right. I was aware of eavesdroppers, and so was Alden. And, true to form, Alden, loving any audience, spoke in a softer than usual voice to ensure that the folks around us would really have to strain to hear him. I helped myself to a few of the succulent clams before devouring my own lunch. Alden began.

"Oh, big deal. Twelve hours? Try that routine for three days. The *Hannah Boden* is an ocean liner compared to what I used to put to sea in. You've been spoiled. Why, I remember a time when . . ." And in the truest tradition of one-upmanship, my friend then painted a picture that made my horror show look like a kid's cartoon. I could feel the bridge ladies perched on the edges of their chairs behind me. George and Tommy had spun around on their bar stools and were leaning toward our table. The suits and ties ordered more coffee, and the islanders knew there would be later ferries home. I had a brief moment of sadness with the recognition of the possibility that stories of the sea might be all Alden had left of his fishing career. The sadness passed quickly as I saw the gleam return to Alden's blue eyes as his story unfolded. Almost everyone loves a sea story. No one tells one quite like my friend.

BAR SNACK

TOP TEN FISHERMEN'S LIES

1. My radios weren't working.
2. We aren't catching anything over here.
3. They didn't look that big when they came aboard. (This is used by commercial fishermen at the dock after unloading big trips on which they used lie #2 on a daily basis.)
4. I'm a purist. I only fish with flies.
5. It's not about killing fish. It's the process and communing with Nature that I like.
6. We're strictly catch and release.
7. If I knew where we were, I'd tell you.
8. If I ever get home from this trip, I'll never go offshore again. I am going to get a real job.

9. We caught them all our last day. Honest.
10. You should have seen the one that got away.

"The one that got away" is universally used by commercial and recreational fishermen alike. Come to think of it, I have never heard anyone say, "I lost the tiniest fish today. Really. It was no bigger than a guppy. It didn't fight at all. It came right to the boat and dropped off my hook."

3

EVEN KEEL

I should say, no one tells a story quite as poorly as Alden does. He can't tell a joke either, although it never stops him from trying. He blurts out the punch line prematurely, and works from there in reverse through the body of the joke. It just does not work. When Alden tells a story, which he does frequently, he takes too many detours and hairpin turns, making it impossible for his audience to follow. Verbally, Alden is always off balance, or "unstable," like a vessel listing to one side or the other, or loaded so that she is top-heavy.

Since befriending me when I was nineteen, Alden has constantly preached his take on stability with regard to seaworthiness aboard a vessel and diplomacy and moderation in "civilian life." There are countless mathematical formulas having to do with the stability of a vessel, both for determining and correcting, and although Alden is well educated and experienced with these, his sound advice is simply to "keep her on an even keel." This advice has served me well through the years, as is evident from the fact that I am still alive and have never lost a boat. Alden's pet peeve at sea is a list, or a leaning of the boat to her side, even slightly, and he's been known to wake a man from a sound sleep to shovel ice from one side of the fish hold to the other to correct the situation. In the middle of the only four hours of sleep you may get for days, this has seemed nitpicky, but Alden's insistence on maintaining a stable vessel in good weather to ensure safety in bad weather is always appreciated when the weather turns bad. In life other than fishing, Alden has been known to say, "Do as I say, not as I do." He expounds moderation in all things and the value of maintaining stability and balance, but his actions are quite the contrary, something that manifests itself in his abrupt manner.

I have always heard that one should never let the facts stand in the way of a good story. Alden's personal variation on that theme is to never allow the good telling of a story to overshadow in any way what you really want the listener to know about yourself. "I hold an unlimited merchant marine license—that's any vessel, any ocean. I was in the Marine Corps—major. I flew jets—A-4 Skyhawk and FJ3 Fury. I was a great baseball player— Ted Williams of Maine Maritime Academy . . ." These are only a few of Alden's sound bites, and he can and will squeeze them into a narrative on any subject. (Alden loves seeing his name in print. I not only have his permission, but also his encouragement, to make him out to be as big a jerk as I can manage; his only fear is that I might say something nice about him, damaging the reputation he has worked so hard to gain.)

In an attempt to spare you, the reader, the agony of wading

through the braggadocious muck that his narrative generally gets mired down in, I have taken the liberty of editing slightly while still trying to reflect Alden's voice and style, and so have deleted some of the expletives and the majority of Alden's extraneous asides extolling his own accomplishments and attributes. For example, I have no reason to think the following needs to be included in a story of bad weather at sea: "When I was an infant, our house caught on fire and my mother stuck me in a snowbank up to my waist while she saved a few worthless personal items, like my sister. No wonder I'm all fucked up." Believe me when I tell you that this type of interjection jumps into every Alden monologue, regardless of topic or who is listening. While these interjections are amusing, they tend to diminish the drama of the story itself.

Another rum and Coke and glass of Chardonnay appeared, sent over by George and Tommy. "Thanks, boys," Alden said, acknowledging the gift by gently raising his glass in their direction. I wondered what the effects of alcohol might be on his pacemaker. Following a quick sip and "Ahhhhh," Alden began his tale, while I continued to munch a few of the golden fried clams from the mound remaining on his plate.

"Let's see . . . where was I? You goddamned kids are spoiled. Nice big boats, EPIRBS, great radios . . . things weren't so easy when I got started. This man . . ." (A signature Alden phrase, he refers to himself thusly while striking his sternum with a clenched fist for emphasis and pronouncing "man" like a Jamaican, odd given that he hails from Orr's Island, Maine.) "This man is one tough motherfucker." The bridge ladies paused in mid-recall of a disastrous spade lead rather than diamond, part of the perpetual act of replaying every hand ever dealt. (My mother can't remember where she put her eyeglasses, but never forgets a misplayed card.) Alden then began to lead us through an ocean storm, perhaps the worst of his forty years of commercial fishing. The reliving and telling seemed to pump new life and enthusiasm into him. His complexion suddenly peaked, even brighter than its usual high color, and I nearly forgot about his weakened condition. As he spoke of an earlier day, the look on his face lightened and his entire physical appearance seemed to have traveled through a time warp, back to a healthier era.

The *Margaret F.* was a 52-foot wooden boat, tough and able. But Alden may have been stretching her capabilities in the early 1970s when he "loaded her for bear" and struck out for George's Bank for a three-week swordfishing expedition. A six-man crew and only twenty gallons of fresh water for twenty-one days meant rustic, nearly barbaric living conditions aboard the tiny vessel. The men lived and worked like animals. The *Margaret F.* was so heavily laden that she was barely afloat upon departure from the dock in Lowell's Cove, carrying barrels of extra diesel fuel on deck as well as a fish hold full to the hatch with ice. By today's standards, anyone in their right mind would have condemned the little craft, and indeed the entire venture, as foolhardy. A few tears were shed on the wharf as the *Margaret F.* melted into the horizon. "No one cried for me, though. In fact, my loved ones only cried when I returned from sea. The newlyweds were always the worst—practically having sex on the dock. Me, I'd rather fight than fuck any day." And at this juncture, Alden gave me his usual lecture on priorities and told me what mine should be. Relationships did not make the list.

When Alden finally found his way back to the story, he and his crew were taking a short nap after having set out the 20 miles of longline gear 200 miles from the closest spit of dry land. "And let me tell you something there, sweet pea, I never had any fancy equipment. I flew by the seat of my pants, and always got a boatload of fish. Imagine what kind of devastation I could have wreaked with forty miles of modern gear and some electronics. Loran A was all we had back then. Didn't know exactly where we were at any time, and didn't have a clue some of the time." The flat, calm evening ended quite abruptly, as did the men's sleep, when Alden got nervous about the velocity of the wind at the crack of dawn and yelled down into the fo'c'sle for the crew to rise and shine. By the time the men had pulled boots and oilskins on and straggled onto the deck, the conditions were severe. "Christ, we had more green water above us than under the keel. Shit was going everywhere—slat, bang, pound. Well, you know me. I wasn't letting on that I noticed the weather. My crew members were products of the shallow end of the gene pool. So, I figured as long as I showed no concern, they'd never have a sour thought. They were good men, though—the best—they'd work in scuba gear if I asked." On and on he went with the commentary of how his crew endeared themselves with loyalty, physical ability, and intellectual shortcomings. You see, Alden knows that he is smarter than the average fisherman, but also understands that the average is awfully low. He won't come right out and tell you that he's a genius; he knows better. But he will go to extremes to depict those around him as numb. I suspected the timing at this point in his tale was right for Alden's well-rehearsed dissertation on Norman, and was not disappointed.

I have known and worked with several Normans; everyone

has. But no Norman can compete with Alden's Norman. "If he had just kept his mouth shut, no one would have known how stupid he was. He was handy, almost clever in some ways. He could fix a lawn mower, which wasn't too useful aboard the boat. He was with me one summer seining for porgies. Right in the middle of setting the purse seine around a massive school, he stopped dead in his tracks. His eyes were the size of silver dollars and he could hardly speak, he was so wrought up. What I understood him to stammer was that he had never seen the moon move so fast. He was amazed! One minute it was on our port side, and the next it was on our starboard! Well, I spent ten minutes trying to explain to him that the boat had come around in a circle and that the moon had not moved, but I didn't convince him. The whole astronomy thing really stupefied Norman. Another time Norman had overheard something about a full solar eclipse and we had to listen to him yammer for days about the 'total collapse of the moon.' Stubborn bastard. If he got a notion in his head, which was rare, you couldn't pay him to change his mind."

Alden chuckled, clearly remembering Norman fondly. As quickly as Norman had interrupted the storm scene, he exited, leaving Alden's thoughts and concentration on the sea story. The weather must have been horrendous that morning aboard the *Margaret F.*, as the next fact that Alden conveyed was that he couldn't get the buoy marking the end of his gear aboard the boat. He tried in vain again and again to get close enough for one of his men to reach it with a gaff, but with each attempt, either a gust of wind would blow the bow off or a wave would push the flag just out of reach. In conditions this rugged, there is no backing the boat down, or lying in the trough. The gear had to be hauled with the boat's bow into the wind as much as possible.

Each time the buoy was missed, the captain had to turn the boat around quickly, steam away from the buoy, and come back to it jogging slowly into the wind and sea that were intensifying with each failed approach. Each approach took a little longer as the boat struggled as if tiring in the battle. Each ditched attempt and subsequent turning around carried the *Margaret F.* a bit farther from the flag than she had been in the previous cycle.

"What a squall!" The spray was like hot darning needles in his eyes. Alden was having trouble seeing and instructed the boys to go below for a cigarette while the system passed. Alden returned to the wheelhouse, where he jogged the *Margaret F.* into the wind, staying close to the flag so as not to waste time finding it again when the weather retreated. The chatter on the CB radio was all about this unpredicted, unanticipated, unappreciated, and unwelcome visit by Mother Nature. Alden was disheartened when he heard the positions of other vessels and what they were experiencing. This was not a squall. This would not pass with the smoking of a single cigarette. Alden's immediate concern was his gear. All of his gear, 20 miles or so, was attached to the flag right in front of him. If he could only get tied into the end, he was sure he could haul it all aboard and then wrestle with the storm. ("Gear" is like "stuff," and can refer to anything from one fishhook dangling from a bamboo pole to enormous winches, wire cables, and nets the size of football fields. Here, gear is the assembly of 20 miles of line and hooks and buoys used to catch swordfish.)

Alden cleared the salt deposits circling his eye sockets with the palms of both hands and tied his oil jacket's hood tightly around his baseball-capped head. He pulled blue cotton gloves onto strong, well-worked hands and yelled to his crew, "Okay, boys. Let's get this gear aboard!" The men were in position instantaneously. Just as Alden was securing the wheelhouse door behind him, he heard his name called over the radio. He stepped back inside and answered someone who turned out to be the captain of the vessel closest to the *Margaret F.* It was a large, steel boat, not far away. In fact, close enough for her captain to train binoculars on the activities aboard the *Margaret F.*, which he had been doing since daylight.

"You're not going to try again, are you, Cap?" asked the man.

"Yes. I need to get my gear aboard. Over."

"Now you listen to me, sonny. The only thing you *need* to do is keep that pisspot afloat and your men safe. From the looks of things where I sit, you'll have your hands full. Forget about your gear. It's as good as gone."

If the man had been within striking distance, Alden might have beaten him senseless. Why didn't that other captain understand that those 20 miles of gear and 400 hooks were what would support these six men and their families? Oh sure, Alden thought to himself, easy for you to say. Forget the gear. You're running that nice, big, company-owned ship. You have nothing invested in that operation but a pair of boots . . . plenty of money for new gear where you come from. Who's going to replace my gear? Alden paused with the mike keyed and looked out onto the deck where six dedicated men lined the rail and squinted unflinchingly into the spray at the flag that appeared to be moving away in slow motion. The boat lurched and the men disappeared in a flood of green water. Slowly, the water cleared, exposing all six men standing and ready, like statues. Not one head turned to another in disbelief or disgust or fear. Not one set of eyes looked questioningly to their captain for affirmation that things were all right. Alden raised the mike to his lips and said, "Thanks for that. Over."

They would leave the gear in the water while they battled the storm and come back for it later. Alden felt his guts dissolve like a stick of butter in a microwave oven, leaving an empty shell as he called his men in from the deck, advising them, "Hang on. We're in for a ride."

The ride was definitely worth the price of the ticket. It lasted three days. There is only so much one can say about a miserable storm at sea, only so many adjectives, so many analogies. Alden's description was similar to any I have ever heard, and reminded me of every hairy situation I had experienced. His tale featured the requisite white knuckles, seasickness, and terrifying sea state. Suffice it to say that the men of the *Margaret F.* had a horrific seventy-two hours. I am sure some of them prayed for their lives; one even cried and accused Alden of attempted murder. The intimate details of people's behavior and conversation in life-threatening situations are, I assume, universal and seldom spoken of. It is within the context of what is not shared in the retelling that the bonds or kinships among people of the sea exist. One needn't be employed as a fisherman to be connected. Anyone who has spent some time on the water has had "an experience" worthy of telling. The Fraternal Order of Salt does not trace lineage in blood, but rather in days and miles on the ocean. In the expressions of the people around us at the Dry Dock, it was clear who was and was not part of the alliance. Some marveled at Alden's concluding comments, while others related and understood. "It's all about stability and balance. The smallest boats can be safe in the worst kind of weather if you keep 'em on an even keel."

In all of the terror that Mother Nature served up during those three days, nothing was as bad as watching the end buoy fade out of sight. The buoy marked the end of the gear in which

Alden had his life's savings and all hope for a successful financial future for himself and his crew. "It made me sick to my stomach," Alden recalled. And he looked ill remembering it these thirty years later. As I now watched the color decant from my friend's face, I was reminded of what my mission for this meeting had been. I almost summoned the courage to bring up his retirement, then thought better of it as he finished with, "I could have thrown up. That flag was tied to everything I had done, all I stood for, and my entire future. I was helpless. For the first time in my life, I felt I was being controlled by something and could do nothing about it. *This man* is one tough hombre, and I could have thrown up helplessly watching my life disappear with that flag end."

BAR SNACK

FIBS AND EXAGGERATIONS OF CREW MEMBERS

1. The Myth of the Decorated Veteran.
   Lying about military service is common. Military service alone is not sufficient material, so these crew members' tales often include wartime participation and stunningly heroic actions. Vietnam is quite popular, with the Gulf War running a distant second. Former Navy SEALs and fighter pilots are abundant on the decks of commercial boats. When pushed for details such as dates and locations of service, the fabricators generally find these specifics too painful to relive, suffering from post-traumatic stress syndrome or the effects of Agent Orange. "I have been trained to kill."

2. The Almost Athlete.
   Narrowly missing Olympic teams due to injury or

blackballing, many of these superb athletes turn to a life at sea. Golden Glove boxers are numerous, as are championship wrestlers who almost made it big-time with the WWF. I once had a deckhand who had been drafted by the Boston Red Sox. He had a hat to prove it.

3. Master of Martial Arts.
Black belts galore! This is nearly a requirement for work on deck. "These hands are registered as lethal weapons."

4. Kingpin of Drug Cartel.
The only reason these men go offshore is because someone is trying to kill them. They leave a huge amount of money (all cash) behind to pursue a life of baiting hooks and gutting fish. "I have Mafia connections."

5. The Self-Proclaimed Genius.
These men turn to fishing because they are too smart for mainstream society. Many of them, members of Mensa, have been subjects of case studies on extreme intelligence. Doctors have no way to measure their level of brain activity. Child prodigies, they dropped out of school due to boredom and the fact that they were always smarter than their teachers. They are overqualified for most work and are generally misunderstood—most of us of inferior intelligence are too far beneath them to "get it." "Do you have any idea what my IQ is?"

4

RUNNING OUT
YOUR TIME

I thought I heard a sniffle from the bar and knew without looking that George and Tommy were well into their cups. They were, I sensed, hanging all over each other and expressing their love for one another, but might just as easily be engaging in fisticuffs with the serving of the next drink. The crying jags were nearly as obnoxious as the fights, and I only hoped that Alden would not be drawn into either. I probably worried needlessly. Alden had, in recent years, outgrown most of the shenanigans that he used to engage in. One night in the "drunk tank" (his term, not mine) at the Portland police station had apparently cured my friend of overindulging. I suspected that doctor's orders may have had some effect also.

With Alden's exclamations of his own tenacity still ringing in my ears, I felt compelled to share a story I thought my friend might enjoy. I got it straight from the source, David Marks. After hearing this tale, I became convinced without question that David Marks, who is in his early forties, is among the toughest, most resilient, resourceful, and resolute people of whom I have ever heard tell. David Marks is indeed even tougher than Alden imagined himself on his best day.

I had coincidentally run into David Marks just one week prior to my lunch date with Alden. David appeared exactly as I remembered him: a big, teddy-bear sort of guy with a very friendly and gentle demeanor. He had added a bit of facial hair, and had replaced oilskins with a crisp captain's uniform, but he was still the soft-spoken, congenial man I recalled singing "Paradise by the Dashboard Light" over the VHF radio one dismal and sleep-deprived night, cheering up an otherwise discouraged fleet of Grand Banks swordfishermen.

During a guided tour of the vessel now under his command, a luxurious dinner boat available for charters of up to five hundred passengers, our conversation quite naturally covered our good old days of swordfishing in years past and found its way to explanations of how each of us had come to where we were now. By the time David Marks had finished telling me the story of his final swordfishing trip and the ordeal that had caused him to change careers, I could think only of Alden and a dead-reckoning navigational term he frequently used, "running out your time." Alden rarely used this term, common among seamen, with regard to navigation, but rather in reference to things more complicated. David Marks had successfully given up a life he loved. Why couldn't Alden? Surely Alden had maintained his chosen speed and course. Time was the last variable in the equation.

• • •

Fishing was David Marks's first love. And he was good at it. When the owners of the longliner he was captaining decided the boat would go to Hawaii, David opted to remain on the East Coast, where he planned to spend more time with his young family. Things couldn't have worked out better for David Marks. He soon landed the captain's position on a 65-foot fiberglass longliner, the *Misty Dawn*. Running the *Misty Dawn* proved to be good duty, fishing relatively short trips around the Caribbean and reoutfitting in St. Thomas, Virgin Islands. David Marks would run the boat for three consecutive eight- to ten-day trips and would then be relieved by the boat's owner for a trip, during which David flew home to Florida to enjoy time with his wife and three children. And, most important, David Marks was catching fish. The *Misty Dawn*'s sword and tuna were receiving top buck because of the freshness that was a result of their spending so little time packed in the fish hold. The shorter the trip, the more value the fish per pound. David Marks did not miss the thirty- to forty-day Grand Banks trips at all. It was great to have a life that included, but was not exclusively bent on, chasing fish.

"It was a dream come true."

Or it was until 1995, a year that sported one of the more active hurricane seasons in recent history. David Marks and his three-man crew had successfully dodged many weather systems already that year, sometimes coming back to the dock in St. Thomas, other times running south to Venezuela, depending on their position at the time and the forecast path of the storm. It had been six years since Hurricane Hugo (a category 4) had devastated the area in 1989, wiping out the fish and fishing industry along with everything else. Now the fish were back in force, and the *Misty Dawn* was taking advantage of the time between storms. (Numerical weather-rating systems have come a long way in the past two hundred years. The Beaufort scale was devised in the early 1800s and ranked conditions from numbers 1 to 12, 12 being a hurricane. The descriptions corresponding to each number were in terms of the behavior of a man-of-war ship in the weather being defined. No wind velocities or wave heights were included. For example, 12 was defined as a hurricane, or "that which no canvas could withstand." Today, the Coast Guard issues warnings and forecasts marine weather based primarily on wind velocities and wave heights; i.e., a "small-craft advisory" is winds of 18 to 33 knots and average waves of 4 feet or higher. Since 1969, hurricanes have been described using the Saffir-Simpson scale, which categorizes systems with the numbers 1 through 5. This scale, rather than being concerned with the behavior of a ship at sea, is used to give an estimate of potential property damage and flooding along the coast from a hurricane landfall. A category 1 threatens unanchored mobile homes, while a category 5 may result in complete building failures and require evacuation.)

Three days into the fishing on this particular trip, David Marks began the all-too-familiar exercise of tracking yet another hurricane. This one, Marilyn, was predicted to travel south of St. Croix and turn to the north over Puerto Rico. Winds were scheduled to reach a velocity of 80 knots by the time Marilyn passed below St. Thomas, blowing the island a kiss; not devastating, just miserable. The boat next door, *Triple Challenge,* was the *Misty Dawn*'s constant companion, and the two captains worked together sharing information and assisting one another in a variety of ways typical of commercial fishing buddies. Both boats' owners kept eyes and ears on weather maps and forecasts and hands on radio microphones to alert their captains and keep themselves aware of the actual conditions being experienced and the positions of the vessels at sea.

"Both owners were really good about staying on top of things."

Radios and cell phones were buzzing and fax machines tapped out weather maps and the men listened and studied and thought out loud. In a conversation with another captain who had secured to the dock in St. Croix, David Marks and his buddy were urged to do the prudent thing and head back to St. Thomas, where each could batten down his boat and hope that in the end he would think he should have stayed at sea. Better safe than sorry.

Soon the *Misty Dawn* was at the fish house in Crown Bay unloading swordfish and everything else the crew could think to off-load in preparation for Marilyn. David Marks stepped onto the scale between the fish. The cook, Cardinal, who was a slight, native West Indian, smiled when he saw his captain tip the scale at 229 pounds and said in a thick Caribbean accent, "The sign of a good cook is a fat captain."

"I've always carried extra weight."

David rubbed his stomach and laughed, shaking his head. The other crew members, Chris and Tommy, took turns on the scale just to confirm that their captain was indeed eating well and that the scale was not weighing too heavily. (Which, by the way, is not usually a concern regarding a scale that will be used to weigh fish to be sold.) Tommy was the first mate and nearly a physical carbon copy of the boss. He did not doubt the accuracy of the scale. Chris, younger and thinner, was a dark, good-looking kid and almost too clean-cut to have any credibility as a fisherman.

"Chris was one of those guys who just didn't look the part. We called him Hollywood. I always thought he would be comfortable in a suit and tie."

Boxes of frozen bait were handed man to man from the *Misty Dawn* to the fish house's freezer; here the bait would ride out the storm. Loose gear, buoys, high-flyers, boxes of spare monofilament, light sticks, and tackle of all kinds were hefted from the boat's deck and stowed within the safety of the building on the wharf. The crew threw the lines off at the Crown Bay fish house and back on at the adjacent Crown Bay Marina as David Marks backed the boat's engine, bringing her to a stop so they could finish battening down for Marilyn, who was bearing down on her predicted track. As the men worked, the harbormaster and some other government official made their way purposefully along the otherwise empty dock and approached the *Misty Dawn* and the *Triple Challenge*. David called out a cheerful greeting that was answered with a serious, "You can't stay here. There's a hurricane coming. You'll have to take safe harbor elsewhere." It is commonly thought that a boat is safer on anchor, where it is free to swing with wind shifts, than being tethered to a dock, where both boat and dock can be destroyed in particularly nasty conditions.

"They kicked us out."

Boats of all types and sizes were anchored in marshes, tied to mangrove trees, and hunkering down in every hidey-hole imaginable. David Marks and his pal, after inspecting the chart, decided to take refuge in a small, sheltered spot called Flamingo Bay, on the end of Water Island. Coral reefs made the entry into the tiny bay tricky, but once inside, both the *Misty Dawn* and the

Triple Challenge found themselves protected by mountains in three directions.

Both boats were secured by two anchors, each with ample chain and scope. Everything was done according to "the book." Fuel filters were changed to gear up for the storm that would soon be passing below Flamingo Bay. David talked via cell phone and radio to his wife, the boat's owner, and captains of other vessels in the vicinity, including a 130-foot Coast Guard cutter anchored just over the mountains in another small bay of Water Island. The captains and crews had done all they could to brace themselves, and now had only to wait for the hurricane to approach and pass, allowing them to go about the business of fishing.

"We were ready. Marilyn was still on her predicted course and at a category two or three in strength."

Figuring that in the worst-case scenario they would be busy for a few hours, and the weather conditions could possibly deteriorate to a state of being too uncomfortable to prepare a meal, Cardinal cooked a huge feast of spaghetti for his captain and shipmates while waiting for the storm to materialize and blow by. Tommy, who read constantly, sat with a book and a cigarette after stuffing the beginnings of a potbelly; Hollywood meticulously cleaned the dishes; and the captain gathered the latest forecast. Usually, waiting for a storm was worse than the weather that had been promised, anticipated, and prepared for.

"Around six that evening, we started to get some wind. Forty to fifty knots, and lots of rain. I was on the radio with a friend named John in St. Croix, and he was getting blasted. The dock he was tied to was going underwater, and he was worried."

It soon became clear that the weather John was experiencing

was coming precisely fifteen minutes later to David Marks. Whatever John reported, David got exactly that in a quarter of an hour. The weather forecast changed slightly. Now the storm would run right over St. Croix rather than pass south of the island. John reported 100 knots of wind, roofs flying off of houses, boats breaking free and smashing into one another and the shore. David now had to engage the engine and run the *Misty Dawn* up closer to the anchors to relieve some of the strain on their lines to avoid dragging them. He had, he thought, about 70 knots of wind and knew, as John was his crystal ball, to expect more.

"John was getting pretty excited at this point. He was still tied to the dock, but his lines were tight and causing the boat to list as the water continued to rise."

The 40-mile gap between the islands of St. Croix and St. Thomas is where Marilyn decided to stop and regroup. She intensified to a category 5, and there was nothing anyone could do but their best to hold position while she gathered steam to move out. John was now in the eye of the storm and adjusting lines before getting hit with the backside of the hurricane. Meanwhile, David Marks was experiencing more wind than he had ever imagined possible. He now had the throttle full ahead to stay up on the anchors, and still the lines were humming tight and threatening to part. He was too busy to talk on the radio or phone, so he had his crew manning all avenues of communication while he fought the wheel. Like a schoolkid with a pencil in both hands, the wind snapped antennas effortlessly. Now the men of the *Misty Dawn* were down to one VHF radio, with which they stayed in touch with the *Triple Challenge*, whose men were also struggling right next door. Two flags tethered to poles in nightmarish gusts of wind, the two fishing boats were out straight on their anchor lines.

"I have never seen anything like it. The wind had whipped the top of the water into solid foam and was throwing it onto my wheelhouse windows. All I could see was a glow from my searchlight."

Then, quite suddenly, the glow disappeared. The *Misty Dawn* went from feeling like she was holding her own in the battle to being pummeled by waves and tossed wildly about. David Marks could feel that they had lost both anchors even without looking at the chart plotter, which showed that they were indeed off station and quickly moving to open sea. Both the generator and main engine had died. No power. The captain ordered his men into their survival suits and went quickly to the engine room to see why his only line of defense had caved. The indications were that both engines had overheated and had been snuffed by the automatic shutdowns. David Marks was able to fire them both back up and see the needles of their temperature gauges move quickly from pegged right to normal positions. Had the boat run aground onto a coral reef? Had the boat been airborne? Had foam rather than raw water been sucked into the cooling systems? David Marks bolted back to the helm, where he knew the power of the 871 Detroit diesel engine was his only tool in wrestling the possession of his vessel away from Marilyn, who was beginning to tighten her fists confidently.

"I fought and I fought and I fought; it seemed like hours. It may only have been thirty minutes."

The pressure was so great that the Lexan windows of the *Misty Dawn*'s wheelhouse became convex, and Hollywood held his handsome head between his hands as if trying to keep it from exploding. David Marks was now contemplating putting his vessel onto a beach, but the radar was struggling to scan against the wind and was only occasionally giving the captain a glimpse of the shore. With so many reefs, cliffs, and rocks in the area, it would be impossible to land on the only sandy beach without the radar outlining the shoreline. And, if they landed against cliffs in this weather, the men would be shredded along with the boat. As David Marks fought to keep his vessel in the water, things sounded chaotic, really desperate, aboard the *Triple Challenge,* which had also broken free of her anchors and was foundering.

The *Triple Challenge* had hit bottom, or been smashed by a wave, and was taking on water and about to roll over. David Marks instructed the other captain to get out of the wheelhouse before his vessel rolled, but the reply was that the boat's mainspool had broken free of its steel bracket, and after slatting around the deck had come to rest against the door, pinning captain and crew inside. David, who was cool under pressure and thinking clearly, reminded his buddy of the main hatch.

"Things were pretty hysterical next door. I could see their lights. I told them to climb out the hatch and that I would come and get them. I didn't know exactly how I would get there, but I would."

The *Triple Challenge's* lights grew brighter and David Marks thought he was making remarkable progress until he realized that the foundering boat was being blown down upon the *Misty Dawn* at some velocity. Now it appeared that the two vessels would collide. "Jesus, they're gonna hit us!" David Marks cut the wheel hard to port in a last-second attempt to avoid an impact with the other steel vessel, and his crew reported seeing four men clinging to the roof of the *Triple Challenge* as it went up on a crest that carried them over the stern of the *Misty Dawn,* which had fallen into a trough; the boats missed each other by inches. In nearly zero visibility, the *Triple Challenge* was quickly blown out of sight.

"I found out later that the winds were clocked at one hundred and eighty to two hundred and twenty knots. I was helpless. All I could do was try to save my boat and crew."

When the *Misty Dawn's* high-water alarms began to blare, Tommy squeezed his broad shoulders into the engine room to see water rising quickly. David grabbed the VHF's microphone and put out a Mayday call that was answered by the Virgin Islands radio operator. The woman efficiently and professionally relayed messages back and forth to the Coast Guard. The bottom line was that the 130-foot cutter anchored just around the corner was also having problems, and that David and his crew would have to abandon ship with the promise that the Coast Guard would come and rescue them after the storm passed. David did not think that abandoning the boat in such severe conditions was an option until his vessel took on enough water to cause her to list at 15 degrees.

"Hell, we were going to roll over eventually, or be pounded apart. So we figured we would take our chances in the life raft."

David Marks and his crew climbed into their survival suits; these are designed and intended to keep their occupants both protected from exposure and afloat. These suits, one size fits all, fit all differently. Cardinal and Hollywood had plenty of extra room in their suits, while David and Tommy struggled to get into theirs. David then informed the Virgin Islands marine-radio operator that he and his crew were abandoning ship for the raft and would be expecting to see the Coast Guard ASAP. The captain shut down both engines and opened the wheelhouse door with the intention of grabbing the raft from its bracket on the roof.

The next thing David Marks was aware of was that he was in the water and his suit was filling quickly, as he had not zipped it up all the way. A splash beside him was Hollywood, who had been sucked right out of his survival suit altogether and had only a life jacket around his neck. As they watched the lights of the *Misty Dawn* disappear, David recalled thinking that the captain was supposed to be the last man off the boat and that this was all wrong.

"The wheelhouse must have imploded or something. Hollywood and I landed one hundred feet from the boat and we had no idea what had happened to Tommy or Cardinal. It was, I guess, around nine o'clock at night when the shit really hit the fan."

The next eight hours (David's best estimate) were all about survival . . . just hanging on to precious life. Again and again, 15- to 20-foot seas crested over and broke directly on top of the two men, driving them beneath the surface with such force that they could not hold on to each other and could do nothing but hold their breath until popping back up, finding each other, and holding on until pushed below again. When underwater, David Marks sensed that he was close to the bottom and splayed arms and legs in all directions in hopes of fending off abrupt contact with the jagged reef. On top, he would gasp for air and get a breath he hoped would last until he popped up again. Sometimes the breath fell short. Throwing up saltwater became part of the on-top ritual for the two men as each wave forced more seawater down their throats and up their noses. Severe cramps were relieved by letting bowels and bladders go. If the weight of 20-foot waves was not enough to damage both body and soul, debris flying and striking at an excess of 150 knots per hour was.

"Coconuts were like cannon balls. It was almost safer below the surface. My suit was protecting me from most of it, but poor Hollywood was getting shelled."

After so many hours of this torture, the men had devised a system. There was a brief calm just before each thrust and dunking, during which the men would lock themselves together in the most stable fashion they could manage. Facing each other with bodies bent in 90-degree *L* positions, they wrapped their arms around each other's lower legs at either side and held on until ripped apart by the water. The time between thrashings was spent getting back to each other and into this position. The men were well exhausted, but the only alternative was to give up and die. Miraculously, they found themselves in the eye of the hurricane.

"It was amazing! I was lying on my back trying to rest up for the other side of Marilyn. It was so calm. It was sort of like looking up through a traffic cone. All these dark clouds swirling around this small, perfectly round, clear spot, with the moon right in the center. Well, we figured we had made it through the worst."

The backside of Marilyn was no picnic, and came upon them with no warning. The wind went from zero right back to screeching. There was no slow mounting of the seas. The waves picked up right where they had left off, steep and powerful. David found himself singing and praying and thinking of his daughter, Maddie. When he laughed, Hollywood wanted to know what was so funny. David Marks explained that his three-year-old daughter was going to get him through this ordeal. His wife, he rationalized, would survive losing him, and his two sons would go on. But not Maddie. She could never make it without her father. David had an image in his mind and held it tightly. He and Maddie were sitting at the table having dinner. She looked at her father with a sideways glance, and when they made eye contact, she laughed. Such a simple image, but the laugh was infectious and caused David to laugh too, and upon the telling to Hollywood, he too chuckled and created his own image. His was of his two nieces. So, it seemed, three little girls would give the men the strength to hang on a bit longer.

The slightest hint of daylight was the men's first indication that they had survived the night. The wind subsided to a stiff 40 knots; not a good day for the beach, but relatively civil conditions. The men felt strangely rested, as if they had somehow gotten some sleep between episodes of near drowning. Maybe it was the sun coming up, or perhaps the feeling of elation that they had escaped death, that gave them a sense of renewed hope. They had, they thought, only to wait to be rescued. As the morning progressed, it finally became light enough for the men to see absolutely nothing but ocean in any direction. They wondered and guessed where they had been blown and washed to. How could they have traveled so far from where they'd started that they couldn't see even a glimpse of land? They knew only from the sun which direction was east.

Now the wind had dropped out a bit more and it was broad daylight. The men took advantage of the swells that lifted them to a vantage point from which they could finally see a tiny speck of land on the northeastern horizon. The island in the distance further confused the men, as they could not imagine being so far from land. If the speck was St. Croix, and the sun had risen in the east, then the men would be right on top of St. Thomas. And they were not. If they had somehow traveled to the north of the islands and were drifting north, as they suspected, then they had a long way to drift before fetching up on Bermuda. David quickly squelched that worry.

"I knew that between my wife and my boss, every possible thing was being done to find me. I assured Hollywood that we would be rescued. It was just a matter of time."

Bobbing and drifting and being slapped by an occasional whitecap, the men heard helicopters before actually seeing them. On top of a swell, they clearly saw two helicopters to the north of their position. Then, sinking into the trough, they had only the sound to reassure them that a search was under way and not far off. Both choppers appeared to be hovering and not covering any ground or growing any closer. They watched as one helicopter descended very close to the surface, and imagined that it must be picking someone or something out of the water. Excited now, the men swam toward the helicopters.

David Marks's exposure suit was full of water and each arm felt like it was being dragged through peanut butter as he flailed and made almost no progress before finally exhausting what energy he had managed to store. Hollywood was in severe pain and in much worse shape than David. The handsome young man lacked both the body fat and the protective suit that clearly were making such a marked difference in the physical status of the men. The life jacket that may have saved Hollywood's neck had also burned a bloodied ring around it over the course of the night. The front of the vest that rode on his chest had chafed the nipples from his breasts and continued to ensure that every movement gnawed skin from flesh with salty abrasion. Hollywood didn't scream out in pain until one of the helicopters sped off in the opposite direction and went right out of sight. The remaining chopper flew closer and closer until it was directly over the men and so close that David Marks could see the pilot's helmet and goggles. The helmet and goggles made a big circle, then flew back to the east and disappeared.

"I couldn't believe we hadn't been seen. We were freaking out."

David Marks quickly pulled himself together and calmed his young crew member, who was in agony and weary to the point of delirium. David convinced Hollywood that the searchers would be back. They had pulled someone out of the water, and would be back to look over the area again. David was even successful in convincing himself, and one hour later back they came. This time it was a plane. A C-130 flew low and slow, again exactly over the top of the two men, and again showed no indication that it had seen either of them. There was neither alteration of course nor dipping of wing. The plane just kept right on a-goin'. Shortly after, another plane did the same thing.

"They were so close to us, we could read their numbers and see that only two of their four props were turning. I could have cried."

But, far from crying, David Marks realized that with every aircraft that passed them over and didn't see them, their chances of being rescued were getting slimmer. This area had been searched quite thoroughly. The current had carried the men a bit closer to the dot of land that, although still appearing to be hopelessly out of swimming range, represented an alternative to waiting to be seen and perishing passively. The weather was now the usual for the area, a fresh breeze of about 20 knots with some of the swells whitecapping. Having agreed that swimming to the island was perhaps their best chance of surviving, off they went as if they actually had some remote chance of making it. Four or five strokes of the crawl just about finished David Marks. Next was the backstroke. The problem with swimming backward was not seeing the next wave that curled over his head. So, the breaststroke was the ticket.

They had basically gotten nowhere when David knew he had to let his suit go. Although the exposure suit had kept him afloat and somewhat protected from the elements, he just could not pull the suit full of water along any farther. He was exhausted. Hollywood agreed to share his life jacket, which was now tied around his leg. The plan was to swim together, taking turns with the life preserver.

"It was a tough decision to let the suit go. But I couldn't think of any other way."

David Marks stripped to his boxer shorts and resumed the breaststroke. He got into a rhythm, ducking his head under and kicking through cresting waves. Hollywood was keeping right up. They were making progress. David sang a variety of songs, and church services came back to him in vivid detail. He remembered who sat next to him and what they wore, and the sermons verbatim. He talked to his pastor. He prayed, like never before. And he sat at the table with Maddie and laughed. The island was now bigger, and a second island appeared. St. Thomas?

Hollywood was getting worse. He had to stop and rest frequently while David treaded water and waited for him to swim again. When the rest periods got longer than the swimming periods, David Marks knew he would never reach land at such a pace. He too was way beyond fatigued, physically and mentally spent. David told Hollywood that he could not wait for him anymore. He told the young man to keep the life preserver that David himself had yet to use, and that he was going to continue to swim to the smaller, lower of the two islands now in sight.

"I told him that one of us would be found, and we could direct the search to the other. I started swimming, and one hour later, I looked back and saw no sign of Hollywood. I kept going."

David Marks swam and swam and swam. He breaststroked through alternating periods of hopefulness and hopelessness. One stroke, he thought the island was growing, and the next, he was sure that it had moved away from him. He breaststroked right past two tiger sharks that were feeding on a dead animal.

"The sharks didn't even scare me. I figured I would punch them in the nose, and if they ate me, so be it. I never missed a stroke and kept my pace. The sharks were so interested in the dog or goat they were chewing up, they never noticed me. I swam right by them and did not look back."

David Marks was now becoming very optimistic about making it to the island. The current had helped him along. In midstroke, he clearly heard a man's voice yell, "What the hell are you doing?" It was his first mate, Tommy. Tommy was so strong, he appeared to be bigger than the island David had been swimming toward. The two swam toward each other, both thinking that they had finally lost their minds. Quickly, they exchanged similar stories of how they had gotten to this point. Neither had seen Cardinal since being blown out of the boat. After seeing the helicopters and planes that morning, Tommy, who wore a life jacket over his T-shirt, had shed his exposure suit in order to swim as David had. Swimming together toward the island, both men wondered if the other was actually there, or if their waterlogged and exhausted imaginations were playing games with them. Not that it mattered. They swam and swam and swam.

Although he'd been struggling and fighting for his life for over twelve hours, David Marks had lost all concept of time and concentrated only on place. And, as relieved as anyone could imagine following this horrendous ordeal, David was elated to know his place was now within striking distance of the island he had focused on since it had appeared as the tiny dot however many agonizing hours ago. Tommy and David were at odds about which side of the island would be best to approach. The island was no bigger than two football fields, but being dry, represented an entire continent of safety. It would not be easy to clamber aboard. Tommy wanted to swim to the north and get ashore in what he assumed would be the lee of surf that lashed and pounded a very formidable-looking coastline. David was all in favor of the closest point, which was now a stone's throw away. So, the two separated, each to pursue his own strategy, planning to meet once ashore. Tommy swam around the end of the island and out of sight while David Marks made his initial approach.

David was so anxious to get out of the water that he planned to bodysurf into the ledges and cling to the side of sheer cliff until a passing aircraft spotted him. The first part of the plan was successful. He surfed right onto the cliff, where he clung to the rock with fingers and toes. The solid rock felt like heaven for the three seconds that he remained in contact with it. As the water rushed back to sea, it ripped David Marks from his perch and threw him into the surf, where he imagined he'd be torn to pieces. Before this could happen, another wave threw him back to the cliff, where the cycle was repeated, this time tossing him away from the island and out of the surge. As David's head broke the surface of the water, he knew he had to go to plan B.

"I thought, Oh my God, I am going to die here after all of

this. I have come all this way, and am going to die right here in the surf, right next to dry, safe land."

Maybe Tommy was right, David thought, and started to swim to the north side of the island. But it was no use. He made absolutely no headway. He swam as hard as he could, but was swept backward.

"Well, I've never been extremely religious, but I was doing a lot of talking to my God. I really think someone or something else was in control right at that point. I spoke out loud, and said, 'Okay. You want me to go the other way? Here I go. You put me through all of this shit, and will not let me get ashore. I have swum through a hurricane, and how many miles, and by feeding sharks, and nearly been shredded on cliffs, and you will not let me swim ashore here. You want me to go this way? Well, here I go.'"

As he swam with the current, the south side of the island was zipping by. The ragged shoreline and surf looked like sure death to David Marks. Then, in the middle of all the white water, David saw what could be his salvation: a small area of calm and thirty feet of beach preceded by a barren of flat rocks.

"I paddled right in there. I landed on a flat rock about twenty feet from the beach and just sat there. Twenty more feet, just four or five more strokes, but I couldn't bring myself to jump back into the water."

Finally, David coaxed himself back into the ocean and swam the four or five strokes that carried him to the island proper, where he stumbled to the side of a cliff over which poured fresh rainwater. He drank from cupped hands and bathed his sun-scorched and weather-lashed face. He drank and drank. He took off his boxers and washed them in the waterfall. He drank and wallowed in the fresh water. His drenched body soaked up the sun.

When he couldn't drink anymore, David Marks climbed back into his boxer shorts and began to pick his way through sharp rocks and cactus plants to the highest point of the island. The going was tough, and his feet hurt, but not enough to stop. Other than some birds, the only sign of life was a goat that David nearly bumped into, startling both goat and man. As the goat skittered off, David again spoke out loud. "You'll be my dinner tonight if I'm not rescued before suppertime." When David reached the highest point of land, he took off his boxers and hung them on the end of a long stick to use as a signaling flag.

"I sat there buck naked for a while just soaking up the sun and wondering. I looked south, in the distance, at the island I believed to be St. Thomas, and wondered."

The sound of a helicopter was music in David's ears. He couldn't see it, but it sounded so close that he got very excited and anxious. He thought maybe he should put his boxers on, but before he could, the tail of the helicopter came around the island, passed well below him, sped off to the south, and was gone. The sound dissipated with it. This brought him to the lowest psychological depth he could imagine any man had ever sunk. Now what? David heard Tommy cursing below him and knew he was not alone. The two men lamented another missed opportunity and then rejoiced in the knowledge that they were both still alive and not in the water. They didn't dare think about the fate of their missing shipmates. It was now late in the day, so it looked as though they would have to prepare to spend the night here. They would be rescued tomorrow, they reasoned.

The men made a bed out of palm fronds. David decided to make use of the last bit of daylight by making an SOS with some loose rocks while Tommy hunted for food. David ran out of rocks and energy after one *S* and half an *O*. Tommy returned with some eggs he had found in a bird's nest, a cactus, and hearts of palm. The eggs made both men vomit, and the juice from the cactus was "gross." There wasn't much in the way of fresh water up on this high spot, but Tommy rolled up a plastic picture holder from his wallet that he somehow still had with him, and the men took turns sucking water held in little pockets in the rocks with the makeshift straw. They chewed some palm fronds, which were not good, but the lesser of all bad culinary options.

The men curled up in the palm-frond bed, huddling together to stay as warm as possible. It began to rain. They were cold. They used Tommy's T-shirt to absorb the rain and sucked the water from it. They shivered. They sucked the shirt all night and talked about the plan for the following morning. At some point, they heard another helicopter pass at a close distance, but figured they didn't have enough warmth between them for any infrared devices to detect their presence.

"The plan was for me to swim to the next island, spend the night, and swim to St. Thomas the next day. Tommy would stay put and hope to be seen by a helicopter. One way or the other, one of us would be saved and could direct the search to the other. Tommy was not in good shape, and I couldn't just sit and wait and hope."

Morning came, and the men talked about the plan. David was having a hard time with the fact that he had to get back into the water and spend two days swimming, but saw no other course of action. They made their way to a spot that looked like a good diving platform that would allow David Marks to land beyond the ever-present surf. They sat and talked while David summoned the courage to dive. David was standing, poised, ready to launch himself into the ocean, when suddenly Tommy pointed to the south. Another helicopter. They watched the chopper travel from east to west and back to the east while slowly getting a bit closer to their perch. They watched and waited and dared not hope. They had been disappointed so many times. The chopper appeared to be searching the other islands. It grew a bit closer and went into its east, west, and east pattern again. It got closer and went around to the other side of the island, where the men could hear it and imagined the sound growing fainter as it left them to die.

Again David stood and summoned the courage to dive. Then the sound got louder and louder, until they saw the helicopter inching its way around the island toward them, its nose pressed almost against the cliff. They began waving arms, life jacket, and even boxer shorts. David Marks could see the familiar black goggles and helmet and read the pilot's lips as he said, "I've got two."

The ending was quite miraculous. After being in the heart of the storm, both aboard the boat and in the water for a combined thirty-six excruciating hours, all of the *Misty Dawn*'s men were found alive. Hollywood was picked out of the water by a helicopter and Cardinal washed up on a beach where local fishermen stumbled upon him and called the Coast Guard. Their friends aboard the *Triple Challenge* were not as fortunate, however.

Alden was clearly moved by this story. I glanced around the bar and noticed that no one was paying attention to our table. I felt the time was as right as it could ever be, and asked, "Do you think you've run out your time?"

Alden looked puzzled for a second and asked, "What are you asking?"

"Do you think you've run out your time? Fishing? There is life without fishing. Look at David Marks. He's living the life of Riley now with the dinner cruises. Don't you think with your health issues, it's time to slow down?" No sooner had the words left my mouth than I wished I could inhale them back.

I am quite familiar with my friend's temper, and he was mad. His face turned scarlet and veins bulged from his neck and forehead. He pointed a stout index finger in my direction, looked me square in the eye, and scolded, "You're giving *me* advice? If you ever utter such nonsense to me again, you and I will be trading time for distance."

BAR SNACK

HIRING CREW

People unfamiliar with the ways of commercial fishing are often interested in learning about this curious profession. Their curiosity usually manifests itself in the asking of many questions. I have found the question most frequently asked of me is how I go about hiring crew members. This inquiry usually takes the form of "Where do you find those guys?" The tone of the question implies that the questioner expects an answer like "under a rock" or "work-release program" or "the state mental institution." My usual response is, "I don't find them. They find me."

Searching for a job aboard a fishing boat is called "looking for a site." A man seeking offshore employment simply scours the docks for suitable-looking boats. Once a clean and seaworthy boat is spied, the man approaches and inquires.

When I began fishing, back in 1979, it was a lucrative business, so it was rare that there was any opportunity for employment aboard the top vessels. Good deckhands were plentiful, and a captain could be choosy when hiring crew. The following is a typical list of questions I might have asked a prospective crew member at the beginning of my career:

1. Do you have any fishing experience? Explain.
2. Are you capable of standing watch?
3. Can you steer a compass course?
4. Are you familiar with radar?
5. Are you capable of the engineer duties?
6. Can you cook?
7. Are you willing to cook?
8. Can you clean fish?
9. Can you manage the fish hold?
10. Can you tie knots, splice line, mend twine?

Well, you get the picture. Depending on what type of fishing was being done, and what position needed to be filled, the hiring was based upon the answers to questions like these and the captain's general impression of the applicant. The captain invariably asked himself things such as, "Is this a man I can work and live with for a number of days?" "Is he clean in appearance?" "Does he talk too much?" "Can he do the job?" If a captain was satisfied that the man was capable of performing whatever duties were needed, and that he would be somewhat compatible, a short list of rules would be presented, and the man would either accept the job or look elsewhere. The rules were simple: usually no smoking except on deck, no drugs or alcohol onboard, and no fighting.

By the end of my swordfishing career, the deckhand pool had

grown quite shallow. The big money was no longer guaranteed, and the best men had boats of their own or had gone on to other occupations. The "warm body" theory of hiring a crew had evolved. The list of questions to be asked of potential crewmen had shrunk to just two:

1. Do you get seasick?
2. Do you own a pair of boots?

Not so long ago, I was working on the deck of my boat when a young man came along the dock and yelled down to me, "Excuse me. Is your husband aboard?" I politely replied that I was not married and asked if perhaps I could help him. The young man apologized for the mistake and asked, "Is the captain aboard?" When I informed him that I was the captain, he was extremely embarrassed and said, "I guess I just blew my interview!" I hired him on the spot.

5

HOLDING A TURN

Yes, I had upset Alden with my suggestion that he think about re-tirement from fishing. Or perhaps what he found disconcerting was that his disciple, who had revered him for his strength, tal-ents, and love for his chosen profession, now saw a slight chink in his armor. Alden would be bothered more by the fact that I had noticed he was a mere mortal after considering him my indestruc-tible and fearless leader all of these years than he would be by sickness itself. Alden sat and thought (something unusual for him), which made me nervous. He was gathering ammunition and preparing to shred me to pieces. I had been on the receiving end of his lashings (always well deserved) on the deck of a boat, and had no interest in being responsible for his coming unglued, or "coming out of his tree," as he would phrase it, right here in the Dry Dock. I would have to change the subject quickly. I looked around the bar for some inspiration.

A young man hurried through the door from the blustery street and greeted Alden with a smile and a handshake. When the man, I assumed a fisherman, asked how he was doing, Alden replied with his usual, "I'm holding a turn." Too young to be familiar with the phrase that originated with the use of a capstan winch, the man nodded, pretending to understand, and headed toward the bar. I knew what "holding a turn" meant, and hoped it was true of my friend. The operation of a capstan winch was quickly becoming a lost art; capstans were now nearly obsolete along the waterfront due to insurance claims for injuries incurred during their use. A capstan is basically a brass drum that is spun around by a hydraulic motor. Unlike modern winches, neither end of the line doing the work is attached to the drum. A man operating the capstan wraps loops of line around the drum, and as the drum turns, it hauls the line and whatever is secured to the other end. Alden was dating himself with the phrase that referred to the allowing of the line to slip around the drum as it turned, moving the object being lifted neither up nor down. Holding a turn was the equivalent of maintaining the status quo, which in terms of Alden's health could be considered a good thing. It was certainly better than going behind. I wondered if Alden realized how old the phrase was and if he ever worried that he too would eventually go the way of the capstan winch. Rather than jump back into the fire by asking, I studied the bar for yet another subject.

It had become that time of day, late afternoon, nearly evening, when a barroom sees a changing of the guard. There were empty tables from which late lunchers had finally shoved off for home or back to the office to tie up loose ends. A fellow named Hugh, who had been holding down the far end of the bar, nodded good-bye, leaving his usual debris: a completed *New York Times* crossword puzzle and a glass from which the last sip of scotch had gone down simultaneously with the last five-letter word. Amazingly, the finishing of both drink and puzzle were always synchronized, giving him minutes to spare before the departure of the ferry back to his home on Peak's Island. Even the bridge ladies had disappeared after painstakingly dividing their check into four separate tallies. The waitress looked a bit irritated as she picked small change between thumb and index finger from each of the four corners of the table. The so-few coins, I suspected, were her tip. She needn't worry, I thought. Soon the heavy-tipping night clientele would fill every chair and bar stool and even stand on foot, crowding her station.

Tommy and George had reached a point of "critical saturation," which required them to make the most important decision of the day: stay until closing, or stumble back to their boats and sleep off the inebriation in time to leave for the fishing grounds when their crews climbed aboard in the wee hours. They thought to themselves, appearing to be in stupors, and then discussion ensued as to what their joint course of action would be. Gravity had taken its toll on a few strands of George's comb-over hairdo, baring one side of his forehead and masking the opposite eye. Tommy's eyeglasses had slid to the end of his red nose. "Well, I'm too damned drunk to walk, so let's have another drink, and if we're lucky, we'll end up doing something worthy of an appearance by the cops and get a free ride to the dock." I did not actually hear George say that, but when two more drinks were plunked down before them, I imagined that's what he had been thinking. Both men were overweight and appeared to be in poor shape. I didn't imagine they *walked* anywhere.

"Those two idiots give fishermen a bad name," I half-whispered to Alden. George and Tommy were always a good diversion, so I used them now in hopes that Alden would join me in a discussion of their many deficiencies, and that the few minutes spent berating the pair would allow Alden to cool down.

"Don't take it too personally, but you're hardly a fisherman anymore yourself. You haven't hauled a trap since Thanksgiving." Alden braced himself for my reply to his attempt to switch to offense. I took a deep breath and conveniently felt myself going into the defensive mode. Full-court press, I thought. Just before letting him have it, I thought again. Alden was right; that's what pissed me off. Here I was, young and healthy, and my traps were all on the beach. My boat was high and dry and would stay that way until April. My seventy-year-old friend and mentor, with his failing health, was still working circles around me. He was certainly doing more than "holding a turn." It suddenly crossed my mind that I may have wanted Alden to stop fishing so that I wouldn't have to feel embarrassed or guilty about his diligence and my lack of it.

"No shit. I'm afraid I'm becoming a responsible human being. I might even start to pay my bills and everything. I'd give anything to return to my usual status of total irresponsibility, with everything I own in a garbage bag ready to be flung from truck to boat." This unexpected acquiescence threw Alden off a bit, and he hesitated before responding.

"How do you think I feel? I love my new boat, but there's not enough man left in this body to fish her the way she should go."

There it was, right out on the table, the lead into the conversation I had been struggling to initiate. Alden had handed it to me on a platter.

"How's the lobstering?" I asked. I had choked! What was wrong with me? I had just blown a perfect opportunity to discuss my deepening concern for my best friend's well-being.

"The fishing is great. The problem is me, my health. I'm just so damn tired all the time." Alden sighed, and gave me the play-by-play of what his daily routine had degenerated to, which went something like this: Got up, went to the coffee shop, went home and back to bed, woke up, went to the dock, slept in the front seat of truck, woke up, took skiff out to boat, crawled into bunk, took nap, woke up, went back to dock, took another nap in the fish house, woke up, went home in time to go to bed. "I would love to have the health of either of them," Alden said, staring longingly at the two drunks, neither of whom I had ever imagined anyone would envy in any way. Until recently, my friend had been a real bull in his ability to work. He was not dealing well with the number of doctors, prescriptions, and procedures he was now forced to integrate into his life. He was getting a bit sad, perhaps coming to grips with his own mortality, I thought. I was disappointed in myself, that I was uncomfortable with the topic I had so desired, and as the waitress delivered two more drinks, I tried to lighten the mood without changing the subject altogether. I recalled visiting Alden in the hospital during his recent stay there.

Alden had been wheeled from surgery back to his room at Maine Medical Center to find me sitting and reading some literature I had found on his bedside table. Alden was alert and pleased that I was there. He had just undergone surgery to implant in his chest what he refers to as his "Dick Cheney machine," identical to that of our vice president, whom Alden adores. The defibrillator/pacemaker was the most recent attempt to regulate Alden's heart after stents and medication had not quite done the job. Unable to find his magnifying glasses, Alden asked me to read a pamphlet about the pacemaker to him. (He was supposed to read it before the procedure, but the fact that he had not did not surprise me.) When I got to the part about sexual intercourse, I thought Alden might laugh the stitches right out of his chest. "Hey, listen to this, Alden. If the defibrillator fires while you are having sex, your partner may feel a slight tingle."

"Jesus Christ!" Alden exclaimed. "That'll be the first tingle anyone's had in some time! My gut is so big, I can't even see that thing. I can barely reach it to pee. Since I got those stents, there's blood going everywhere, I think. I haven't actually tried. Call the nurse!" We shared a much-needed laugh then, and another now at the Dry Dock. As Alden's laugh slowly subsided, he began to look quite somber again. In another attempt to get myself off the hook, I continued.

I reminded my friend of the time when (during a previous hospital stay) three nurses had barged into his semiprivate room and demanded his roommate tell them Alden's whereabouts. The monitor at the nurses' station indicated that Alden's heart had stopped, and there was some confusion as to why he was not in his bed. The roommate declared that it was not his turn to babysit, and used the remote control to turn up the TV's volume. Some sort of red-alert, STAT, all-points bulletin was announced, and a search party found my friend in the hospital's kitchen, where he was making himself a sandwich. "Well, I felt weak and thought I needed food." Thanks to behavior like that and his now-constant "How 'bout a little tingle, honey?," Alden was assured of never remaining in the hospital one second longer than the medical staff deemed absolutely necessary.

We shared another laugh. That was enough to get us started talking, and soon I wondered why getting to this point had been so difficult. We were conversing just as naturally as we would have been had we been discussing the weather. We talked for nearly an hour. Occasional moments of silent contemplation were comfortable. Alden shared his genuine concern that he might not live forever, and we hashed over dreams and plans that he had not yet accomplished, with the unspoken understanding that some of these might die with him. Alden confessed easily that he was unsure how much longer he could hold a turn. We did a good job of talking about mortality, but not such a good job of getting to practicality, like how long Alden should go on fishing. As the bar again reached full occupancy, Alden grew uneasy with the seriousness of our conversation and quickly changed the subject. "How's your buddy Archie doing?" Alden asked in reference to a friend with whom I had just enjoyed a visit.

"Oh, he's great. We went fishing one night for swordfish with rods and reels. It was a blast. And he told me this really creepy story that he said had been haunting him for years, and now it's haunting me."

"Haunted? Like ghosts?"

"Yes."

"Give me a break. Haunted? Have you ever seen a ghost?" Alden sounded disgusted with me.

"Well, no," I answered. "But I've never seen the Grand Canyon either, and I don't doubt its existence." And even though skepticism was oozing from every pore of his skin, I decided to pass the haunting along to Alden, as Archie had done to me. Maybe I could scare him into taking a break from the water. When Archie told me this story, he'd handed me a file folder of newspaper clippings on it. The contents of the folder weighed no more than a loaf of bread, but were strangely burdensome. I now considered the possibility that my objective in lunch with Alden might partly have been to get some things off my chest and ease my mind rather than his.

One clear and cold winter day in 1980, Arthur Jost, also known as Archie, found himself killing a little time while waiting for the ferry to Shelter Island. Archie, in his mid-forties, was as Scandinavian in appearance as his family name would suggest. However, his dialect and accent were all Montauk, New York. This stocky, blond, blue-eyed native of Long Island was also 100 percent fisherman. As he walked along the shoreline, stopping briefly to skip a rock, his mind was cluttered with all the details of the two-week fishing trip he would embark on the following day. Archie had been longlining sword and tuna for some time now, and knew the importance of being organized, well prepared, and fully supplied. He stared seaward and wondered where this fishing adventure would take him and how many fish he would land.

Walking along the beach between ocean and wetlands, Archie first ignored the chill on the back of his neck, which bit easily through the sunshine. The chill became a tingling sensation that crept inside his collar and down his spine, where it soon caused him to shiver. He faced the ocean, allowing the sun to beat directly on his back. He sensed something behind him, something deep in the bulrushes. Now Archie had to concentrate to not allow his thoughts to be distracted from the pending fishing trip. As he turned to wander back toward the ferry landing and run through the mental list again, that same something drew him closer to the cattails. He peered through the growth, and was surprised to see the skeleton of an old wooden vessel embedded therein. So there *had* been something behind him. Strange, he thought, how compelled he was to inspect the remains. Marine surveying was one of dozens of pies in which Archie kept his fingers, so it was natural for him to satisfy his curiosity. But this was different. "Something came over me. I know how weird this sounds, but I was physically drawn to the old wreck."

Archie carefully picked his way through the dank marsh and was further intrigued as he approached the skeleton. The bulk of the remains were deeply embedded in brush and weeds, a clear indication that the vessel had died long ago. But the outside hull ribs extended well beyond the intertwining growth, like giant fingers stretching in anguish from a premature grave. This was too creepy. Archie took a step back, slipped, and automatically reached out his hand to grasp one of the ship's wooden ribs to break the fall. He hung, suspended, until the wooden rib cracked and snapped off in his right hand, dashing him to the ground. Archie scrambled to his feet and rushed back to his car, tossing the rib piece onto the backseat. He then raced to get his car on the ferry.

All during the ferry crossing and drive home to Montauk Point, Archie's imagination was racing. He tried, but he could not escape the questions raised by the six-inch piece of wood. What type of vessel was it from? How did that ship end up in the wetlands? How long had it been there? Why had he felt drawn to it so? Upon his arrival home, Archie had so much work to do that he was able to put all thoughts of the ship aside. He laid his souvenir rib on a coffee table and got busy. Exhausted when he flopped into bed that night, he fell quickly and deeply to sleep.

Somewhere in Archie's ascent to the surface of consciousness from the soundest sleep, a blue light appeared in his mind's eye. The light grew bright, then dimmed, grew brighter still, and faded again, over and over, pulsating like a heartbeat. At its faintest and palest blue, the light spread across a large diameter; as it intensified in brilliance, it became a cobalt pinpoint. It seemed to be getting closer, or clearer, with each throb. Now in the broader, dimmer flashes, faces appeared, one face with each cycle. The faces were urging Archie to some action, but he didn't understand what the strangers wanted.

Finally it all stopped and Archie lay awake thinking about what a weird dream he had had. Probably just need to use the bathroom, he reasoned. And up he got to stumble to the toilet through the dark. No need to turn on the lights, he thought; no need to wake up his wife, Marge, or himself for that matter. As he walked through the living room on his return to bed, he crashed into the coffee table with his right shin. He tried to stifle a scream as pain shot down from his shin to the top of his foot. He hopped around on his left foot for a few seconds, and then alighted on the sofa. His foot was killing him and he thought he felt a trickle of blood run down into the arch. Switching on a table lamp, he saw that his foot was indeed bleeding. The rib from the wreck lay on the floor now. He had knocked the rib off the table and its sharp, freshly broken end had stabbed him. He reached down and picked up the rib from the carpet and cradled it in both hands. Suddenly Archie felt totally and completely connected. The strange dream, the overwhelming feeling of intrigue at the site of the wreck, and now the rib; he vowed to himself to uncover the mystery of the skeleton ship.

When he returned from his fishing trip, Archie devoted himself to research. He soon discovered that the rib was from the remains of a charter fishing boat named the *Pelican*. The *Pelican's* last voyage was on September 1, 1951. It was the last voyage for many of the souls on the *Pelican* too.

September 1, 1951, would be a big day, and John Griffin could hardly sleep, he was so excited. A bricklayer from Brooklyn, New York, John and his wife, Josie, had driven to Montauk the night before and slept in their car to ensure that they would be the first in line to board the *Pelican* for a fun day of fishing. The sun had not yet risen, and soon the "Fishermen's Special," a train run by the Long Island Railroad from New York City to the dock known as Fishangri-La, would roll in with hundreds of anxious fishermen who would rush and crowd aboard the boats making up the charter fleet of Montauk Point.

The *Pelican* was the most sought after of the boats in the fleet. She was 48 feet in length and had twin engines and a reputation for putting fish on the dock. "I'm not going," Josie informed her husband just before stepping aboard. She had had a dream of disaster, she said, in which the boat had flipped in a storm and everyone had died. There was no time to reason with her. The crowd had arrived and now was pushing and shoving to get spots on the most popular boat. John elbowed his way aboard, leaving his wife on the dock. He hadn't the time to explain to Josie that the New York State Conservation Department had determined that there were over one million fishermen in New York alone, including women and children, and that fishing was far safer than driving the highways on this holiday weekend. The operators of the Montauk Point fleet had an outstanding record for competence, seamanship, and ensuring the safety of the passengers.

At her 48-foot length, the *Pelican,* along with the others in the "head boat" fleet, was well under the 64-foot minimum—this meant there were no federal statutes restricting the number of passengers she was allowed. "Head boat" meant that payment to the boat owners was by the head; so, the more heads, the more money. Captain Edward Carroll was as good a fisherman as any, and was known to be very conscientious with regard to his equipment and the well-being of his customers. Crowding, though, was another matter. He thought nothing of the near fistfights among people in their attempts to get aboard his boat. There's always room for one more. This was just another day for Captain Carroll. The sixty-five happy folks who managed to squeeze aboard were no different from the sixty-five who had experienced a wonderful day of fishing the day before.

The mate threw the lines off the dock, and away they went, heading for the Frisbie fishing grounds south of Montauk Point. Ninety minutes later, they had just reached the grounds when the light southeasterly winds swung to the north and began to blow hard. Other boats were heading back to the dock, many of their customers seasick and frightened. Captain Carroll announced that he would do the same even though some of the anglers begged him to remain at sea. They had been looking forward to this trip for weeks; most had come here by train, and some had even slept in their cars. For the sake of safety, the captain knew to head for the barn with the others.

Among the boats that cut the day's fishing short was a cruiser out of the Edgewater Yacht Club, the *Betty Anne*. The boat's owners, Roger and Jeanne Bishop, had taken Jeanne's parents and a friend out to try their luck with tuna. As they were trolling just out of sight of land, at about 11:00 A.M., the sky darkened with ominous-looking clouds and the wind perked up to a degree that convinced the fishing party to haul in all lines and go home. Within thirty minutes, the waves had grown to 20 feet in height, forcing Mr. Bishop to run toward Block Island and then tack back in the direction of Montauk, their ultimate destination.

As the conditions worsened, the folks aboard the *Betty Anne* were quite anxious and felt relieved finally to see Montauk Lighthouse. Although the worst lay ahead of them, the sight of the lighthouse was reassuring. Just off of Montauk Point, where the ocean and sound come together, the riptide creates a confused sea, unpredictable and dangerous even in less extreme weather. Bishop later recalled in a newspaper account, "Instead of the mountainous swells, it seemed as though some giant was pinching the water into gigantic individual peaks, with no rhyme or reason to their formation and no alternative but to wallow and batter our way through it." So, wallow and batter they did. They wallowed slowly and painfully by the *Pelican*, whose "sides were black with people."

Aboard the *Pelican*, the port engine had refused to start, so the captain was heading toward the dock on just the starboard engine. It was slow going and the weather had gotten worse. Now many of his clients were feeling queasy, and some huddled in the cabin for warmth. As the *Pelican* rounded the point for Montauk Harbor, the riptides were raging. With just the single engine, she lacked the power to make way and rolled relentlessly. Only a half mile from shore, she seemed to be stationary. More folks were sick now, and more found room inside the cabin to huddle and anticipate the glorious dock. John Griffin had fallen asleep sitting up jammed between two other passengers. Suddenly awakened by a slamming wave, John decided to don a life preserver and go outside for a breath of air. The other passengers jeered at him and called him a chicken when he pulled the preserver over his head. He said that he was not scared, just careful.

The next wave was a monster, rolling the *Pelican* nearly onto her side. Before she fully recovered, another wave blasted her and she capsized. John Griffin was swept away from the vessel, along with everyone else who had been on her deck. Onlookers from shore called the Coast Guard, and two privately owned boats, one being the *Betty Anne,* raced toward the scene to help.

The Bishops had actually watched the *Pelican* roll over. They had seen her struggle, but noted that "she was gamely fighting her way toward port." The next dip and rise revealed only the *Pelican*'s keel, onto which clung twenty people and at least as many heads were bobbing around in the cold, rough seawater. The *Betty Anne* was close enough for her passengers to hear the screaming. Mr. Bishop spun the *Betty Anne* around and headed toward the capsized *Pelican* while his crew gathered life jackets and lines to assist with the rescue. Simultaneously, another charter boat, the *Bingo II,* responded. Both boats' crews were now throwing life jackets to free swimmers and bobbers, and hauling victims aboard with lines. "Several other boats were downwind from the wreck but apparently were tossing so badly that they could not come in. Then we were horrified, as we pitched and tossed like a cork, to see that the *Pelican*'s keel had been swept nearly clean of people and only the stern was sticking above the waves. Those that we thought were fairly safe were being widely scattered in every direction."

The difficulty of maneuvering the *Betty Anne* in such conditions was now magnified as the Bishops hauled aboard the first victim. The man had only enough strength to hold the end of a line the Bishops had tossed and could not help pull himself over the *Betty Anne*'s side and into the cockpit. The waves flogged the man against the side of the boat until one advantageous sea helped lift him over the gunwale and tumble him into the cockpit. The screams coming from the water were getting fewer and fainter as the temperature and horror of what was happening both shocked and weakened those who had survived this long.

The next person, also a man whom the Bishops rescued, had his arm wrapped around his lifeline when it got fouled in the *Betty Anne*'s propeller, nearly drowning him as it sucked him under. The crew worked quickly to clear the line, haul the man to the surface, and wrestle him onto the deck. "He shot into our churning wake, his rope fouled into the propeller, and he was dragged under as our pilot threw the gears into neutral and stopped the wheel. The next few seconds, or minutes, or hours, were a nightmare of cutting ropes, gunning the motor, pitching and tossing, getting the man to the ladder, which one of our party descended and finally boosted the helpless man aboard." They were next able to pull aboard a young girl and boy. By this time, all other previously bobbing heads had disappeared, so Mr. Bishop headed for the *Pelican*'s keel, where three people were hanging on for dear life.

The size of the waves and the intensity of the wind made it impossible for Mr. Bishop to safely sidle up to the overturned *Pel-*

ican. He made several nearly suicidal attempts before one of the three people waiting to be rescued leaped and swam toward the *Betty Anne.* From the stern of the boat, a line was tossed and caught. But a following sea pushed the victim quickly toward the *Betty Anne,* resulting in a slack loop in the lifeline, which naturally got sucked into the propeller, stopping it and jamming the rudder to boot. To add to the panic, the person they were trying to save had become tangled in the slack and was now under the boat. "No one can picture those frantic moments in the trough of the sea, nor the relief of finally getting free, pulling the man onboard, and drifting far enough from the wreck to be safe from the hazard." There were now two Coast Guard boats on the scene, and the only victims in sight were the two remaining on the *Pelican's* keel, and the body of a woman who had succumbed floating nearby.

The drowned woman was one of forty-six dead in the final tally. The long-anticipated day of deep-sea fishing had become a terrible tragedy. Bodies were recovered over the course of several days. When a diver went into the cabin of the mostly submerged *Pelican,* he found a dozen corpses twisted and contorted, "locked together like wrestlers as they died fighting to get out."

John Griffin was one of the nineteen lucky survivors, and the main source of many newspaper accounts. His wife, who had been frantically watching her worst nightmare unfold from the shore, greeted him as he arrived at safety still wearing the life jacket that no doubt had saved his life.

I suspected all that remained of the *Pelican* tragedy was the folder of discolored newspaper accounts Archie had collected and given to me. Why this particular incident affected me so, I couldn't say. Perhaps it was the unfairness of it all. Those innocent people out for a day of fishing . . . it wasn't as if they were tempting fate by working on the water every day, like Alden. I have lost many friends to the fishing industry, and although I miss them, their deaths are shrugged off as part of the business. As I finished telling the story, I noticed that Alden was somewhat distracted, or perhaps he was just lost in his own thoughts. "What were you doing in 1951?" I asked.

"I was just figuring that out. I was sixteen years old, so I must have been going to school and working in the stern of my father's boat. The *Pelican* story reminds me of the *Don*. The *Don* was an old rumrunner converted to a head boat after the Eighteenth Amendment was repealed. My father actually picked some dead bodies out of the water following that disaster," he said. "It was the same type of thing, too many people aboard a charter boat. Odd, so many fishermen go down at sea each year and we quickly forget about them. But a boatload of tourists die, and it leads to investigations and legislation and new Coast Guard regulations. We're sitting here talking about the *Pelican* and the *Don* and you hadn't even been born yet!"

Alden and I were on the same wavelength, which was pretty unusual for us. I thought of all the combined years that Alden, Archie, and I had spent at sea, and we were all still alive to share stories about those who were not. "You're right," I agreed. "You could drop dead aboard your boat tomorrow and your death would be considered part of the territory. Other than a few tears at your funeral and lingering anecdotes, you'd be history. Hell, I'm your best friend and all I'd worry about was whether you had willed me your boat! You are leaving it to me, right?" I teased.

Now the old man was laughing hard. His eyes welled up and he wiped one with the back of his calloused and weathered hand, catching a tear before it rolled down his cheek. "Don't put your boat on the market yet. I'm not going anywhere soon. I'm holding a turn."

BAR SNACK

"The only thing worse than the feeling that you are going to die is the realization that you probably won't."

REMEDIES FOR SEASICKNESS

1. Fresh air.
2. Stare at horizon.
3. Eat saltines or fresh ginger.
4. Keep busy. Mind over matter.
5. Drugs.
6. Wristbands designed to apply pressure.

An old friend of mine once said, "If you've never been seasick, you ain't been there." In this context, seasickness is a rite of passage and something to be proud of rather than embarrassed by. If you haven't heaved your guts out over the side, you just aren't salty enough. You are unworthy of the title "sailor." Well, I've "been there," and although it's been years, the memory of how bad I felt is still fresh. I understand that women forget about the pain of childbirth with time. No one forgets a bout with seasickness. It's worse than your worst hangover, by far. And a combination of the two maladies is deadly. Bed spins and gale warnings . . . it's not pretty.

Aboard a commercial fishing boat, "the green guy" is the new, inexperienced hand and should not be confused with the seasick man, although quite often they are one and the same. I have, in my experience, seen only two cases that I would consider "chronic." In each of these cases the victims were sick from the time they boarded the boat until the moment they stepped back ashore thirty days later. I believe that if either of these two sick deckhands could have mustered the energy to kill either me or themselves, they would have.

6

STAND ON OR GIVE WAY

Although Alden and I agreed that our memory of many fishermen has faded quickly after they passed away, there is a clear exception—Harry Ross. Harry was one fisherman my friend adored and respected, and I knew that the time was now right for Alden to remember him. As long as Alden was alive, the legendary Harry Ross would never die.

"That Harry Ross, what a piece of work. I loved that guy. 'Rules of the Road' be damned, Harry's was always the privileged vessel. He didn't yield to anyone or anything." Now Alden was showing his vintage again by using the phrase "privileged vessel," which had long since been changed to "stand-on vessel" in the U.S. Coast Guard's navigation rules, known officially as "The Rules of the Road." According to the Rules, any time two vessels are at risk of collision, one vessel is the burdened or give-way vessel, and the other is the privileged or stand-on vessel. Alden, who has a habit of putting everything in nautical terms, especially likes to apply "The Rules of the Road" to human behavior. One of the most poignant lessons Alden had worked to drill through my skull was the necessity of knowing which vessel you are; do you back down, altering your course and your speed to avoid collision, or do you hold your own, standing your ground? It's one of the most difficult and important life lessons to figure out.

Harry Ross is remembered frequently around Portland, and any session of sea stories includes a few in which Harry stars. The thing that most endeared Harry to Alden was the stubborn streak they shared. Alden was rarely in a mood to "give way" in any social situation, and truly admired that in his old friend and fellow fisherman. I always enjoyed Harry as a topic of conversation, and joined Alden in rehashing all we knew and then some. Many who surrounded our table pulled chairs close and added what they knew about Harry Ross. When I finally got the floor to myself, I launched into my own favorite sea story.

I began my commercial fishing career in 1979. More notable in that year was the disappearance of Captain Harry Ross. Harry Ross, it was rumored at the time, had skipped town to avoid an indictment on charges of smuggling marijuana. I had never met him, but in the late '70s, stories of his participation in a major pot-running operation were as plentiful and colorful as the fishermen who shared them.

In May 1979, Captain Harry Ross and two crew members put to sea aboard the fishing vessel *Karma,* leaving from a dock in Rockland, Maine. Steaming offshore and into international waters, the *Karma* rendezvoused with an old, rusted coastal freighter of about 140 feet in length. As Harry approached the freighter, he saw that another fishing vessel was nestled alongside it, which meant the *Karma* had to wait her turn. And wait she did, for several hours for the transfer of a full load of marijuana to the other boat. As the other boat pulled away from the freighter, Harry carefully secured his vessel alongside the larger vessel like a feeding young animal to its mother, attached at the hip. The weather conditions had deteriorated by this time, resulting in slight damage to the *Karma*'s hull. Waiting for ideal weather was not an option in this situation, where hundreds of thousands of illegal dollars had to be kept on schedule to make all well-organized connections; the more time hooked to the mother ship, the greater the risk of being caught.

Harry's two crew members worked for four hours loading the approximately 20,000 pounds of marijuana, from freighter to fish hold, that was reported to have been packaged in 70-pound bales. The rectangular bales of compressed cannabis were wrapped in burlap and plastic, keeping them contained and protected from saltwater and other elements.

With the load secure, the *Karma* headed to Portsmouth, New Hampshire, to close this link in the smuggling chain. Traveling at night with no running lights, Harry sneaked up the Piscataqua River, signaling the bridge operator with a flashlight to open up and let them pass. Even the lights at New Hampshire's State Pier had been doused by the time the *Karma* tied up alongside. Everything went like clockwork.

Longshoremen worked quickly and quietly with strong backs and a forklift on the dock as the men aboard the *Karma* hustled to empty her hold of all cargo. Four nervous hours later, a pair of tractor-trailer trucks pulled out and headed off on Interstate 95 as the *Karma* slipped back out to sea for more conventional fishing. Miraculously, she returned to her homeport of Portland, Maine, two days later with a slammer trip of fish aboard. Harry had managed to catch as many fish in two days as his peers caught in a week, giving him an almost perfect alibi. No one would be the wiser. A full fish hold was nothing unusual for Captain Harry Ross, who had literally become a legend, known all over New England for his uncanny ability as a fisherman. His acumen in that regard was truly remarkable, even if his judgment (and, some would add, morals) was not.

In 1979, the marine scientists of the world had just begun to chant what has since become a mantra: They claimed that their studies, formulas, and models all indicated that fish stocks had been significantly depleted and that some species were actually endangered to a point near extinction. There was a corresponding general panic about who was responsible and what should be done to save the fish. Harry Ross acted as a thorn in the side of every government official representing every agency whose job it was to manage or monitor the fisheries and fishermen.

The federal government engaged in a policy of "reduction in effort" for the fisheries, which is (one would think) self-explanatory. Plans were legislated and set into motion to reduce the effort of fishermen on targeted species determined to be in decline; the idea was to kill fewer fish. As the effort to harvest fish was reduced through regulations (including ones that mandated fewer fishermen, closed areas, quotas, and various gear restrictions), the corresponding "landings" (pounds of fish caught and sold) went down as well. Unfortunately, smaller landings were seen by many as evidence that efforts needed to be reduced further, totally frustrating fishermen who could be heard saying, "But I thought that was the idea. Less effort . . . smaller landings. . . ." (This is, admittedly, simplified and opinionated.)

Then there was Harry Ross. Harry Ross outcaught all of his contemporaries, delivering whopping loads of fish with a grin that implied, "Who says there's no fish!"

From what I had heard around Portland's waterfront, Harry was singled out by the enforcement arm of the federal agency whose responsibility it was to police commercial fishermen and ensure compliance with laws regarded by many as aimed to kill the industry rather than make it stronger.

(I'm sure I will be misunderstood here. Regulations were, and still are, needed. But when you've been in the fishing industry as long as I have, and witnessed the injustice of certain regulations, it's difficult to not be cynical. There are bad regulations. For instance, daily quotas on certain species, which result in the throwing overboard of dead fish, do nothing for conservation or for the rebuilding of stocks. In fact, they're wasteful. And another example is the mandatory "weak links" in lobster-fishing gear. This law's purpose is to save right whales when and if they happen to swim into and become entangled in the "vertical lines," the lines that run from trap to buoy. Problem? No right whale has EVER been sighted in the area where I fish, let alone become entangled in a trapline. So, the expense and frig of rerigging gear to make it whaleproof pisses fishermen off. And it winds up lessening fishermen's confidence in the system. I'm sure many readers are getting their backs up, thinking about how fishermen have been raping and pillaging our oceans for centuries, and that more regulations are long overdue. Relax. That side of the coin gets plenty of press in places that are far more widely read than this paragraph will be. My point again: Good regulations are good; dumb ones are not only dumb, they make it harder for fishermen to make a living. The result is that an entire community and way of life are in peril too.)

Suffice it to say that Harry became the poster child for all New Englanders (not only fishermen) who worked uncomplainingly in the face of obstacles. While other fishermen attended meetings, rallies, and protests, Harry was fishing. While lawsuits were being filed, lobbyists hired, and politicians greased, Harry fished. The thousands of tons of fish going across the scales from the *Karma*'s hold did little to promote the idea of more restrictive regulations. The enforcement branch had been told that regulated species were in serious decline, and they took their jobs seriously, as of course they should. Harry became the focus of much attention. To some, he was pillaging the sea; to others, he was proving how robust it was. In the end, one could argue it either way.

Both Coast Guard and fisheries officials frequently boarded the *Karma*. Harry was under tight surveillance not just when he landed a trip but also while at sea. Keeping Harry on a short leash only frustrated the officials as the *Karma* continued to land record loads while playing by the fishing rules. In spite of all the checking, surveying, boarding, and spying, no fishing improprieties were detected because none had been committed. With all eyes on him, what would have tempted Harry Ross to engage in anything as illegal as dope smuggling? Harry surely must have been making an adequate living catching fish. Maybe the lure of breaking one huge law while following dozens of smaller ones was just too appealing.

The irony was that Harry wasn't caught, he was ratted out, or at least that's the way I heard it. Although most people do not approve of smuggling pot, when Harry disappeared to avoid arrest and a prison term, the cry around the waterfront was like "Run, Forrest, run!" Most fishermen are conservative and do not like drugs or smugglers, but everyone loved Harry. Harry stood for an era of freedom that was slipping briskly away. He was our Butch Cassidy and Sundance Kid rolled into one. Harry loved what he did and was the undisputed best. This was a source of inspiration for many who have struggled, barely surviving tough economics and the myriad new laws passed over the last twenty-five years. Many fishermen have been enticed to run drugs for financial reasons. Smuggling marijuana was an act of sheer desperation for most who did it. And because of mandatory sentencing, many fishermen are spending time in prison, while murderers are freed. But the general consensus is that Harry Ross could never have been forced to do anything solely for money. Still, after he split, wild rumors circulated about the vast sums he had tucked away.

When I first began fishing, many young fishermen boasted about having "started with Harry," meaning that they had learned the business from the one heralded as top dog. But by 1986, seven years after his vanishing, Harry was just another sea story. The young men who had worked on deck for Harry now had their own boats full of young men who hoped to someday sit in the captain's chair themselves, a typical progression.

My first captain position was in 1986 aboard the *Gloria Dawn*, a vessel Alden had purchased with my captaincy in mind. I ran the boat for two painful years. I didn't mind being broke; money never held my interest. But such a high percentage of my bad memories are tied to that boat that any other hardship I have ever endured pales in comparison to that two-year stretch. To this day, whenever I find myself in an emotional funk, I simply recall 1986, and am soon back to my cheerful self. The only other good that came out of my tenure as captain of the *Gloria Dawn* was that it was the boat that helped me meet the fugitive Captain Harry Ross. The more I think about it, the more I'm certain that making Harry's acquaintance is the single bright spot in my bleak recollection of that GD *Gloria Dawn*. By meeting Harry, I gained bragging rights that would stand in countless rounds in countless bars.

My voyage to Harry began when Alden finally announced that he was selling the *Gloria Dawn,* and that he would find another boat for me to captain once it was sold. I could hardly contain my excitement! I helped show the vessel to prospective buyers, answering questions but never volunteering anything—by strict order of Alden. I never mentioned the number of times and height to which the water had risen in the engine room. I didn't inform tire kickers of the propensity of the lazarette to flood to the hatch, or of the slight electrical problem that sent jolts from certain pieces of equipment to any hand that touched them. "Hell, it's only twelve volts. Toughen up" was Alden's reply to my pleadings for repairs. (I hoped the new operator would have something in common with Pavlov's dog.) I certainly did not share the story of Uncle Paddy, my cook who had passed away onboard in midtrip and spent ten days in the freezer. Although I was tempted to boast about the boat's refrigeration system, using Uncle Paddy as an example to the man shopping for an "ice-cream boat," I bit my tongue. After all, the quicker the boat was sold, the sooner I would be free to find another site.

Even without my freezer testimonial, a fellow named Bob

Keagle decided the *Gloria Dawn* would make a fine island-hopping, grocery-delivering freighter to join his small fleet down in the Caribbean. I was hired to deliver her to St. Maarten, an island that forms the northeast corner of the island frame containing the Caribbean Sea. I was fairly excited about the 1,500-mile trip and set out to hire a crew. Hiring a delivery crew proved even tougher than I'd imagined, given the *Gloria Dawn*'s reputation. A destination like St. Maarten in February, a free trip south, a paid position, an exotic boat ride, accommodations, food . . . it was no use. I had, over the course of two years, employed nearly every available able body in Portland. And those whom I had not, had heard about our many botched outings from hundreds who'd left the boat wishing me luck and meaning it, as they were surely certain I would never return from the next trip.

James Galvin was a great friend and an exceptional shipmate. Perhaps the only middle-aged man I have ever met with a face of freckles, "James the Irishman," as he was known around the waterfront, had worked with me on several trips aboard several different vessels and was always a pleasure to be around. (Except while on dry land, when he could become somewhat of a nuisance, making me question the "dry" part of that phrase.) James was a good cook and savvy fisherman with a delightful demeanor. He was a fantastic storyteller and had experience fishing around the globe. James had the gift of gab and is one of the more intelligent and well-read people I have ever been acquainted with. James was so drunk the day I shanghaied him from Popeye's Bar to serve as my delivery crew that I became particularly impressed by his ability to forgive once he realized what boat he was aboard and that we were out at sea. I had steamed into the darkness with an unconscious mate and a deckload of odds and ends to be delivered with the boat, including a large scallop dredge for some friend of Alden's named Henry Rich.

James came to just in time to throw the lines ashore at the dock in Provincetown, Massachusetts—at the very end of Cape Cod. The *Gloria Dawn*'s generator had died a sudden death during our first night at sea and P-town was the closest port for a quick repair before we continued on our journey south. I explained to James what the plan was, even managed to convince him that he'd indeed been in favor of, in fact enthusiastic about, the trip the night before when he'd readily agreed to come along and work as both cook and mate in exchange for some much-needed sunshine upon arrival. P-town would be a slight detour, but we'd soon be soaking up some sun.

The slight detour turned into a seven-day ordeal. Provincetown's harbormaster would never have been confused with the welcoming committee. In fact, I have never felt so unwelcome in my life. James and I were treated like lepers. We were initially greeted with, "You can't tie that thing up here." We moved the *Gloria Dawn* three times in the first six hours at the whimsical command of this nasty-dispositioned man who clearly relished his crumb of authority. In time we realized that we were the only ones paying any heed to the harbormaster's orders. Therefore, he wasted no demands on any other vessel, captain, or crew, all of whom we learned referred to him as "the dickhead." The *Gloria Dawn* became the man's personal chess piece.

It was cold, rainy, and off-season for this tourist area. The generator mechanic did not show up the first day. He also failed to make an appearance on the second day. Late on day three he showed, diagnosed the engine's problem, and left to "get a part." Anybody but James would have defected, abandoning me. But

James, being the loyal guy he is, sat with me on the dock, keeping me from becoming totally depressed by talking about other misadventures we had shared in the true "things could always be worse" spirit that cheers one up in this kind of situation. We dreamed about how beautiful the Caribbean would be should we ever actually land there. Oh, and we were penniless. That may have been the main reason we could do nothing but sit forlornly on the dock in the rain. Our options were few. We joked about perhaps selling the scallop-dredging rig intended for Henry Rich or pawning some other piece of gear not needed for the cruise, and the joking helped warm our damp spirits.

As it continued to rain, we continued to wait for the mechanic to return and also to shift the *Gloria Dawn* to different berths at the harbormaster's fancy. This whole trip was beginning to smell like a fiasco. James and I knew all about fiascos. We had shared many. "This isn't so bad, Miss," began James. (James always refers to me as "Miss.") "We could be in Southwest Harbor with that bollix." I had to laugh as we recalled the details of a fishing trip we'd made years before aboard the *Walter Leeman Sr.,* a boat also owned by Alden. Alden was in a pinch and had asked us the favor of going as crew with an unknown captain he had hired who could not seem to scrape up any help of his own. We didn't actually do much fishing.

The captain somehow (and it still amazes me) managed to wrap the main wire (⅞-inch steel cable used to drag the net over the ocean floor) around the boat's propeller. Well, we frigged and frigged, but it was no use—we could not clear the propeller. The captain, frustrated at this juncture, gave the order to cut the wire off and splice the bitter ends back together. He then disappeared to his bunk, leaving James and me (both inexperienced dragger-men) to carry out his orders.

Getting slack enough in the wire between the propeller and the drag that lay on the bottom was a bit of a chore, but we finally managed. The acetylene torch was a mystery, but we had at least *seen* steel cut with a torch, so eventually we were able to keep the flame shooting long enough to gnaw sloppily through the wire. We were feeling a sense of accomplishment now, and really hoped the captain would spare us the embarrassment of trying to figure out how to splice wire. We both knew how to splice line, but splicing wire is a totally different deal, and much more physically demanding. I decided that James should go wake the captain from his "nap" (Rip Van Winkle had some competition here) and have him teach us to splice wire so that we would know how to do it in the future. James returned to the deck and explained that the captain said to "just put it together somehow. It doesn't have to be perfect," and began to snore again. And perfect it was not. But, being as it was "together," we woke the captain next with the announcement that we were ready to continue the fishing.

We made several relatively short three-hour tows for just about nil in the way of pounds of fish. I learned on subsequent dragging trips in the months that followed that the fathoms of wire lost to the propeller would have accounted for the poor fishing, as we never remeasured nor remarked the remaining wire to ensure both sides were even. So, the net was more than likely being dragged sideways rather than with the opening or mouth forward.

Worse than the fishing was the tongue-lashing James and I received each time the net was set or hauled, as the "fucked-up" splice traveled in and out of our view going onto the winch or overboard. I was not born knowing how to splice, and did not enjoy being ridiculed along with James every time the "bird's nest" reared its bungled head. We prayed for the end of that trip.

Eventually the vibration caused by the wire remaining in the prop got so severe that the electronics were threatening to jump from their brackets in the wheelhouse. The whole boat shook as the net was towed askew, catching absolutely nothing. A shackle literally bounced on deck like a kid on a trampoline. As mad as I was at Alden for shipping me out with this fool, I could not stand by silently as he destroyed my best friend's boat. When I shared my unsolicited opinion that we should head home for repairs before permanent damage was done, I was surprised to hear "Good idea" from the captain. James and I were jubilant, secretly planning to jump ship the second we touched the dock in Portland. Also to my surprise was the fact that we headed for Southwest Harbor—not our homeport of Portland. Shit!

While we waited for a scuba diver to come inspect the problem, the captain made his way to the nearest bar and proceeded to drown his sorrows. The diver used three tanks of air before finally clearing the wheel. Now the captain was so drunk, he could not have navigated his way to the men's room from his bar stool, so we went nowhere. James and I, penniless as usual, hung around the boat and paced the dock, cursing Alden for persuading us to step aboard in the first place. After forty-eight hours of cursing and pacing, James and I decided to hitch a ride back to Portland and be done with it. I thought I would at least call Alden and let him know the whereabouts of his boat and that we were bailing out, and when I did, he said, "You leave that drunk behind and bring my boat home, now!" So, that ended up being our first delivery job. And here we were some years later, on another delivery at the hands of Alden, sharing stories of trips gone bad, a list that might well include our present venture.

"We both vowed to never step foot aboard that boat again, and the next thing I knew, I was spending Christmas with you on her deck," I reminded James.

"Oh, Miss! That was the most dreadful holiday." James was right, as I recalled. Again, it was my buddy Alden's idea that led to the less than joyful Yuletide. Alden thought it would be smart to fish over Christmas, as most boats would be at the dock, their captains and crews home celebrating with family. The scheme was to land fish just after the holiday—receiving astronomically high prices—with fat paychecks compensating for missing all the holiday cheer and festivities. James and I, both having no lives, signed on as crew. We were the only suckers Alden could find, but he spun the situation of "going three-handed," rather than with the usual five-man crew, as intentional, pointing out that the pie would be divided into fewer pieces. So, James and I enthusiastically threw our sea bags aboard in anticipation of a gluttonous helping of pie.

Things weren't going badly until about 8:00 p.m. on Christmas Eve. Sitting at the galley table watching James smoke a filterless cigarette and baste the turkey for the last time before dinner, I felt the boat lurch slightly. The lurch was followed by a shout from the wheelhouse above. It was Alden barking, "Haul back!" This is the cue to the crew to hustle into oilskins and boots and get out onto the deck to assist in hauling the net from the bottom of the ocean, depositing its fishy contents onto the deck, and setting the net back out to tow again. Once the net was back overboard, the crew was to "rip and gut" (clean) the fish and ice them into the fish hold below the deck.

James and I scurried into foul-weather gear and stepped from the warmth of the fo'c'sle into the cold, windless night. Bright deck lights lit the working area, sending psychological heat to an otherwise frigid landscape of steel machinery. Immediately, James and I noticed that only one of the two main winches was turning, spooling its length of ⅞-inch wire cable up to pull the fishing gear toward the surface. The wire on the other side had "parted off," or broken, which accounted for the lurch and hasty haul-back order. "Hauling back on one side" is not highly unusual, but calls for extra care and attention once the net surfaces. When hauling back on one side, after the net and accompanying gear (roller frame and doors designed to keep the net open and hugging a smooth bottom or bouncing over a jagged one) are all spun up onto the "net drum" (a third drumlike winch that hauls and stores the net and roller frame), the broken wire and accompanying second wing of the net are still dangling over the stern and need to be wound up onto the drum on top of the net that surfaced before them. Before the broken side (which could be of any length depending on depth of water fished and where in that span the wire broke) can be spooled aboard, the "cod end," or very end of the funnel-shaped net where the fish accumulate, must be secured or "tied off" to what remains overboard to ensure it comes back off the drum at the proper turn. If the cod end is allowed to flop freely with each subsequent spin of the drum, it's nearly impossible to set the gear back out without some major frigging. When hauling back *normally,* both sides of wire come up together and both wings of the net and ends of the roller frame do the same. The cod end would be the last thing to come aboard. The cod end would be popped open, the catch spilled onto the deck; the cod end would be closed again; and the net set

back out. Easy. The whole operation is really not complicated unless you are hauling back on one side and you forget to tie off the
cod end, which is exactly what happened this Christmas Eve.
That creates a god-awful mess and tangle.

Sitting on the wharf in P-town in the cold rain, waiting to re-
sume our trip to St. Maarten, we shivered not so much from the
present weather as from the memory of those long hours dealing
with the snarl on the *Walter Leeman's* net drum so many years
ago. No, that was not a good Christmas. James, Alden, and I
worked through sunrise and the next sunset to get the mess
straightened out while all the other fishermen on the planet cele-
brated the holiday in their toasty-warm homes. It was a mistake
none of us would ever forget. By the time we solved the giant net
puzzle, the Christmas turkey was done to the nth degree and a
storm had moved up the coast, forcing us to the dock prematurely and ending the trip before any money was made. "We didn't
even catch enough to pay for the groceries," I recalled. James
laughed and marveled at how and why either of us had remained
in the fishing industry given the number of bad experiences we
had endured and could bring to mind with such ease. Why? It's a
question I suppose all seafaring people have occasion to ask themselves. It was now clear that Alden had been involved in, if not responsible for, the lion's share of the wretched times we now
laughed about.

The generator was eventually up and running and James and
I left the harbormaster with no one to boss around and growl at;
we hoped to reach our destination before something else broke.
We steamed for a few days in bad weather, making little headway.

When we reached a position south of Bermuda, the wind relaxed, the sun came out, and every few hours brought a few more degrees on the thermometer. Now in shorts and T-shirts, we thought ourselves quite clever and fortunate to be escaping the Maine winter for a while. In spite of the seven-day delay in P-town, which had resulted in a serious hit to the groceries, James and I had a delightful passage to St. Maarten. When the weather is perfect and everything runs smoothly, days at sea are like nothing I have experienced ashore. The ocean has a way of swallowing your troubles, leaving you with a carefree feeling, while at the same time enforcing the notion that you are indeed the master of your own destiny. So, if you are making any headway at all toward a desired destination, you become so content that you dream of staying offshore forever.

The simplest things became astounding. The commonplace became remarkable. The glow of the solar-powered moon and stars held a warmth I'd never known, and wind-generated ripples trickled over the ocean's surface as coolly as spring ice over a ledge. Meals prepared by James were simple—mostly rice and beans—and were vastly enjoyed thanks to the state of mind we both were in, which in turn was thanks to a vessel behaving exactly the way she should. The *Gloria Dawn* was on her best behavior, so much so that I secretly felt bad to be delivering her to a new home.

This delivery was prior to the days of a GPS (Global Positioning System), common now on boats of the *Gloria Dawn*'s size. The *Gloria Dawn* was equipped with the GPS's predecessor, a satellite navigator that periodically got a good fix on our position when it could acquire signals from a certain number of satellites; its ability to do so depended on orbits and weather conditions. The system was less than reliable, and we would frequently go several hours without a fix. This isn't a problem when running offshore, but it can make life a bit difficult when you are approaching land—especially when it is unfamiliar territory to boot. Fortunately, I was accustomed to not knowing for sure where I was for days on end, so did not get nervous when land suddenly showed up on the horizon and in the radar screen. I should have been able to get a bead on my location by picking up signals with the boat's radio-direction finder, but that piece of equipment had been destroyed when a disgruntled and intoxicated crew member had smashed it with a sledgehammer months before.

I learned my dead-reckoning skills from my father when I was a young girl, and after quickly consulting the chart, became confident that the first land I saw was Anguilla. I had been keeping track of compass, speed, and time since leaving Portland, Maine, and getting a good fix from the satellite navigator just often enough to confirm that we were indeed on course. The navigational chart I had been plotting our progress on showed St. Maarten south of Anguilla and a clear and easy passage if we went east of both islands and then rounded up the south end of St. Maarten and into the harbor of Philipsburg. I actually enjoyed the slight apprehension of not knowing *exactly* where I was at every second of the trip, thinking of ancient mariners and people of the sea who depended on the sextant and sounding lead. The more time that passed without a good fix from the electronic aids, the more I contemplated the days of yore when mariners used celestial navigation to find their way even in the fog. The radios didn't have much range, so we hadn't heard a scratch or a peep in days, which was really nice, and a contribution to my ongoing fantasy that I was living my life a hundred years earlier and surviving brilliantly by my wits and the stars.

Big, round rocks loomed on top of the sea ahead. Inspecting the chart, I saw an outcropping labeled "Cows and Pigs." Watching the depth come up, I pulled the throttle back to a safer speed while I got my bearings again from the chart. Finally, the satellite navigator beeped, signaling that it had acquired a good position. I noted latitude and longitude, found exactly where they intersected on the chart, and was relieved to see that we were indeed where we should have been and where I believed us to be. We hadn't far to go now to Philipsburg, where we would be met by the boat's new owner, Bob Keagle.

Philipsburg, St. Maarten, is the main harbor of the Dutch side of the island that is owned by both France and the Netherlands. The Atlantic Ocean cools the northern shores of St. Maarten, while the south side is bathed in the Caribbean Sea. As we crept closely by more rocks, the south end of St. Maarten opened up like a pair of arms poised for a welcoming hug. We must have appeared as ruffians in our ragtag-rigged bleach bottle to all the curious eyes watching us from the large and beautifully manicured yachts anchored forest thick ahead of us. With the heap of spare gear included in the sale of the boat piled high on its deck, and odds and ends lashed everywhere, I imagined we looked like a seagoing *Sanford and Son*.

As I carefully steered through the anchorage, I left the doors on either side of the wheelhouse fastened open to allow a draft to ventilate the un-air-conditioned bridge. Through the doors I could hear shouts from the decks and cockpits of nearly every vessel we slipped by. "Hey! You finally made it!" "Welcome to St. Maarten." "How's the weather in Maine?" So, it seemed most everyone in this transient community had been expecting us a week ago, and James shouted back appropriate responses from the bow where he readied the anchor for a splash.

The water was a distinctly different color here in the harbor, and as the depth shoaled, the color paled from a true, deep aquamarine to a lighter, greener effervescence, like tinted tonic water. I could see the white, sandy bottom clearly at 30 feet. Amazing, I thought. At home, when bottom is visible, it's too late. And it's never sand, but rather dark seaweed-covered ledges that are most unforgiving when they make accidental contact with keel or propeller. Just as I was to give James the signal to drop the hook, an outboard-motor-powered skiff approached, and as it came alongside, I recognized its driver as the tall, handsome, and bearded Bob Keagle.

Securing the skiff's painter with a long loop through a scupper and over the gunwale, Bob climbed aboard and joined me in the wheelhouse. Local knowledge is always appreciated, and it was now Bob's boat, so I was happy to have him direct me to the spot he thought best for anchoring the *Gloria Dawn*. James released the anchor. The splash was followed closely by links of chain ticking sharply over the length of plastic guard, a short but grand welcoming drumroll. I reversed the engine, backing down slightly while James allowed the anchor line to slip through his hands, paying out scope until Bob gave the word to make it fast. James cleated the line as I knocked the engine into neutral.

Bob was telling me how nice it was to finally see us as he quickly stripped to his jockey shorts. I didn't know where to look. This man, a mere acquaintance, had just undressed while talking and now stood in the wheelhouse wearing nothing more than his underwear. Totally unaccustomed to having this effect on men, I would have been more nervous about this unexpected behavior had not James made his way aft and up to the bridge. Before I could say, "What the hell!," Bob stepped out the starboard door and dove overboard.

I suppose I looked a bit bewildered, confused, and dumbfounded, and stood there with my mouth agape, hands on hips and shaking my head. James laughed and said, "He's setting the anchor, Miss. Look," and he pointed beyond the bow at Bob, who was now below the surface and pushing the anchor deep into the sandy bottom. Bob stayed under for what I considered too long for human lung capacity. When he popped up, he swam to the skiff, climbed into it, swung a leg over the *Gloria Dawn's* gunwale, and stood on deck dripping and talking with James. I, meanwhile, had brought his clothes from the wheelhouse in case he had any desire to put them back on. It seems that setting the anchor by hand is quite common south of my neighborhood. Who knew?

A dripping Bob Keagle then told us that the final papers had not yet been completed for the transfer of ownership of the *Gloria Dawn*. He had been in phone contact with Alden and the lawyers involved in the closing, and it had been decided that I should remain in Philipsburg, staying aboard the boat as a caretaker until all matters were settled. This was no hardship from my standpoint, as I was in no particular hurry to return to Maine and I was being paid on a daily rate until I boarded the plane headed north. James, on the other hand, would be given a ticket out of town effective immediately. It was obvious that two of us were not needed to baby-sit a boat at anchor, so one of us would be cut from the payroll. James was handed his walking papers—a one-way nonrefundable ticket home for a flight departing the following day. Bob Keagle soon left with his clothes under his arm. He kindly arranged for us to borrow a skiff to shuttle ourselves back and forth from boat to town.

James was none too happy about the travel arrangements. He stared at the ticket, gazed at his new surroundings, then back at the ticket again, shaking his head in disbelief. "For fuck's sake, Miss! A full week in miserable P-town—and just twenty-four hours in paradise?" I agreed that the deal sucked and promised to see what I could do about exchanging the ticket for a later departure, as James had been kind enough to make the delivery trip, never once complaining, only looking forward with bright thoughts to some time in the Caribbean. James seemed optimistic that I could rearrange his travel plans, tucked the ticket into his back pocket, and buzzed off in the loaned skiff to "explore," promising to return soon so that I might also go ashore.

As the Irishman disappeared among the boats in the distance, another skiff appeared from the direction of town. The skiff came closer and closer until it landed alongside and its driver, its sole occupant, cut the motor. An eccentric-looking man with a shock of white hair and bushy mustache to match stood in the skiff, holding the *Gloria Dawn*'s gunwale to keep from drifting off. Strange, I thought. This visitor had not so much as acknowledged my presence on the deck he was now perusing. "Hello," I said when the silence became awkward for me.

"Hi," was the reply that did not require even a glance in my direction. Very odd, I thought. This stranger had come along quite purposefully and now stood in his skiff eyeballing the mound of cargo stowed on deck. My first greeting upon arrival is from a middle-aged male stripper turned Mark Spitz, and the next person I see is obviously insane. Now the crazy guy concentrated on the scallop drag quite intensely. I was certain that he was trying to figure out what it was, as it would be unheard of in this area of more primitive fishing and harvesting techniques. He squinted, nearly closing his eyes. His head bobbed slightly and I could hear him calculating under his breath something mathematical. Just as I was about to ask how I might help him and shoo him off to bother someone else, he opened his eyes, sprang aboard nimbly, and extended his right hand for a shake. "I believe that's for me," he said, motioning in the direction of the drag.

"Oh, you must be Henry Rich!" I was relieved to be making some sense of this encounter and wondered why Alden hadn't mentioned that his friend was a weirdo.

"Yeah, whatever . . ." And his attention drifted around the boat, mostly up in the rigging. He looked at the things that only real boat people notice and made comments about the *Gloria Dawn* that struck me as highly intelligent and knowing. Alden had mentioned only that Henry Rich was likable, which I now could see. I helped him hoist the drag aboard his skiff using the *Gloria Dawn*'s mast and boom and hydraulic winch. He invited me to have dinner with him and his girlfriend aboard his big boat, which was tied to a dock in another harbor. I readily accepted the invitation, as I suspected that James might not come back for me right away and I was anxious to get off the *Gloria Dawn* for a while.

Dinner was delightful. Henry's girlfriend was the most beautiful young woman. She was from one of the islands south of St. Maarten. He introduced her as "Belky," short for Eubelkis or something like that. She spoke English with an accent that was attractive, but tough for me to understand. She was shy. She clearly adored Henry, which endeared him to me for some reason I do not quite understand. The dinner conversation was really more of a Q and A session. Henry couldn't seem to get enough information about Portland, Maine. He interrogated me about fishermen, fishing grounds, fishing gear, and fish in general. Each morsel of information I gave him was like a crumb to a starving bird. He knew the loran bearings of every piece of bottom in the Gulf of Maine and on George's Bank. When he finally hesitated in his debriefing to take a breath, I asked, "Are you originally from Portland?"

He smiled for the first time since we'd met and said, "You don't know who I am, do you?"

"Henry Rich, right?"

"Have you ever heard the name Harry Ross?"

"Holy shit!" Henry Rich was Harry Ross. Here I was sitting and having dinner with one of "America's Most Wanted," the legendary Harry Ross. I was stunned. I didn't know whether to be thrilled or frightened, so I was both. Harry had been on the lam for seven years and yearned for contact with and news from home. He confessed to me that although he had avoided the secret agents who had come close on several occasions, he might just like to turn himself in, do his time, and be done with it. Which is sort of what happened some months down the road.

As I looked around the Dry Dock, I felt as if I had become the queen of it. This encounter with Harry Ross would be a hard act to follow, and all who listened sat and thought while I added the details necessary to finish the story. James surfaced in two days, long after his flight had departed, with the tops of his feet sunburned to a crisp. He had fallen in love with a bartender, which was quite convenient given his thirst. I had been having coffee with Bob Keagle and some of his business partners at an outdoor beach place when I spotted the Irishman stumbling along the shore. I prayed, "Please, do not let him see me." But, of course he did see me, and joined us at our table, where he picked the creamer from the table and drank its contents. After breakfast, James and I were escorted to the airport and sent home. When we changed planes in Puerto Rico, James disappeared (not a surprise) and I landed in Portland without him.

Of course I couldn't mention to anyone other than Alden that I had met Harry Ross. No one would have believed me anyway. And I certainly didn't want to betray my charming dinner host. I couldn't talk about it until Harry called one night to say he had been caught and was on his way to Maine to stand trial. Everyone sitting and listening at the Dry Dock knew the end of the story. Harry went to prison for a few years, and when he was released, he went about his life fishing out of his home of Portland. Belky came to live with him and they soon had a little baby. Sadly, Harry died not long after the baby was born. He was lost at sea when his boat went down in bad weather.

Alden took a deep breath and wiped what I thought could have been a tear from the corner of an eye, although I tried hard not to notice. "Harry Ross died doing what he loved and never gave way to anything he didn't believe in. There's no truer mark of a man than that. We should all be so lucky." I knew that if Alden could write the ending of his own biography, he'd script it similarly. My feelings for Alden were as deep as his were for Harry Ross. Given all I had learned from my friend, I figured the best thing to do now was to take the role of the Give-Way Vessel and allow him to Stand On. At least for a little while.

BAR SNACK

A BAD DAY FISHING

I recently saw a bumper sticker that read "I'd Rather Have a Bad Day Fishing Than a Good Day at the Office." Although I have never spent a day, bad or good, in an office, I think I can safely say that most folks I encounter have never experienced what I would call a truly bad day of fishing. Sure, people get rained on, or have jerked a fly into the back of their own head, or have drifted with a broken outboard motor right through happy hour. And everyone has spent an entire day on the water without a single scale to show for it. However, I can think of many times when, if the owner of that bumper sticker had been with me, he would most likely have gladly returned to the office. Now, I do not mean to sound like Alden here. I do not have a superiority complex with fishing strings attached. I will now take this opportunity to describe my idea of a bad day fishing. Actually, it's a brief description of my buddy Ringo's worst day. It's always nice to know that no matter how bad your day of fishing, someone else had it worse.

In January 1988, Ringo (Tom Ring) was working in southern waters on the deck of the swordfish longlining vessel *Canyon Explorer*. The boat had been issued a permit by the government of the Turks and Caicos Islands to fish an area within their zone just north of Haiti. While hauling gear one sunny morning in the Caicos Passage, the *Canyon Explorer* was illegally boarded by a party from the Bahamian Defense Force vessel *Yellow Elder* and escorted across the border into Bahamian territory. Under the watchful eyes of two Bahamians armed with nine-millimeter machine guns, the *Canyon Explorer*'s captain was ordered to follow closely behind the *Yellow Elder*, whose captain had set a course for Nassau. In spite of the fact that Ringo's captain warned the Bahamians of his vessel's draft, they managed to put him hard aground on coral reefs twice, and then had to pull him off with a towline.

Upon arrival in Nassau Harbor, Ringo and company were greeted by three hundred special enforcement officers and members of the press. After securing their vessel, the five American fishermen were ushered off to jail. Processed, fingerprinted, and put in a 7-by-4-foot cell that "smelled like the men's room at the Boston Garden on game night," the men were never notified of their rights, nor were they allowed a phone call.

The following morning, the men received a visit from a member of the U.S. embassy who could not tell them what charges had been filed, if any. This official seemed to have little concern for the group's plight, and even failed to make phone calls to next of kin, as promised. The men spent five nights in this fifteen-cell facility in which there was one toilet that did not flush and was "scooped out" once a day. They were so cramped in their space, they could barely sit, and no one slept. The only source of light was from a single bulb that hung in the corridor, casting just enough light into their cell for Ringo to see an army of ants devour a spider the size of a fifty-cent piece. They were fed toast and coffee twice a day, and "mystery burger" each noon. They were finally charged with "poaching in Bahamian waters" and advised to plead guilty.

Five guilty pleas resulted in a fine of $12,000. A U.S. attorney charged another $12,000, the Bahamian lawyer grabbed $10,000, the *Yellow Elder* got them for $7,000 for the towing job, and a miscellaneous fee of $5,000 was added, for a total of $46,000 for their freedom, from an offense they did not commit. Now that's a bad day fishing.

7

NAVIGATION

As proud as I am to say, "I am a fisherman," I often wonder why. I have lived like a nomad, I swear like a pirate, my income has been sporadic at best, and I can look my best friend square in the eye and unflinchingly lie, sandbagging or exaggerating the day's catch. And it's not only the quantity of fish that gets twisted, it's also the location where they were caught and the type of gear, bait, and technique I found successful. Hell, I have even been known to stretch the weather report to my advantage! Mastering falsehoods is not requisite for becoming a "good" fisherman, but most of us have learned the hard way not to share valuable information. If you tell your buddy about a secret and productive spot, rest assured he'll be there the next time you arrive, catching more and bigger fish than you did, and he may not be alone. Before you know it, the entire fleet will be drilling your spot, which may have already become known by some nickname having to do with your buddy and nothing whatsoever to do with you. So, off you go in search of a new spot, kicking yourself all the way. The lesson learned is to deceive, or to at least withhold information. Alden told me this countless times before I figured it out myself.

Fishing has provided the bulk of my incidental education, and other than giving me a flair for creative fact reporting, has taught me many life skills and a value system some judgmental people might regard as somewhat sleazy. I suppose that the textbook definition of fishing, "the catching of fish for a living or for pleasure," adequately describes the activity—for most people. However, I find that simple explanation lacking. Without delving too deeply into the metaphysical, or becoming too Hemingwayesque, suffice it to say that fishing can be a lot more than killing fish, or torturing and releasing them. For a few hard-core types, like Alden, fishing is life. There is nothing else. This puts Alden in an exclusive and tiny group of people who take fishing to such an extreme, they are totally intolerant of folks who claim the status of "fisherman" but do not devote their entire lives to the pursuit of fish. I often use my knowledge of Alden's sensitivity on this subject to get him riled up. When I refer to my five-year-old nephew, Aubrey, as a fisherman, it really pisses my friend off, so I do it as often as possible. And he goes absolutely insane when I call Aubrey's brother, two-year-old Addison, a fisherman.

Oddly, Alden has never been a good liar—at least not with regard to fishing. To keep from having to try, Alden learned to avoid the radio. "Ask me no questions and I'll tell you no lies" doesn't come into play when you don't even afford anyone the opportunity to ask a question. To my credit, with the state-of-the-art electronics, including communications systems, aboard the boats I have captained, "You're breaking up" or "All four radios weren't receiving" just doesn't cut it. So, becoming a good liar has become not only a challenge for me but also a necessity. As I've said, half-truths and exaggeration are expected and accepted practice among fisherfolk—be they commercial or recreational.

In fact, most fishermen revel in their lies. The "one that got away" will get bigger with each telling, while the one in the cooler is not worth mentioning, especially to anyone with an empty cooler. In this, and other ways, I am sure, the fishing industry resembles corporate America. Business ventures seem to thrive on secrecy until a deal is successfully closed. So much of life's interactions, personal and professional, are a balance of said, unsaid, implied, denied.

Parents teach children that lying is bad, but honesty is not always the "best policy," and that is usually lesson number two, immediately following one of Junior's loud observations: "That lady is wicked fat" or "My dad says you're a moron." We make sure that kids know that little white lies are often preferable to the truth. For example, most people consider fibs fine when they are intended to spare someone's feelings. ("Dear Aunt Sally, Thank you for the socks. I love them.") Fishermen lie to protect their livelihood and pride, but also purely in the interest of entertainment. How to find the delicate balance between truth and fiction, and how to know when the truth is unkind or inappropriate, is best taught to children when they are young, and can be relayed most enjoyably and satisfactorily during a day of fishing. Recently, I was witness to my nephews' education by their parents, my brother Charlie and his wife, Jen. The first lessons came at 5:00 A.M. one July day in the downstairs bedroom of my home. Several others followed.

I decided to tell the tale of my nephews' incidental education to Alden in order to drive home my point that anyone engaged in any attempt to catch a fish is, in my mind, a fisherman. And to show that you are never too young to lie.

Charlie, Jen, the boys, and their chocolate Lab, Tucker, were excited to have a long weekend on Isle au Haut with their aunt Linda. They had left from Portland the previous afternoon, putting jobs, preschool, and day care on hold for three days of fun. The parents, to ensure a peaceful three-hour drive from Portland to Stonington, where I would pick them up in my boat, gave both children heavy doses of Dramamine under the guise of motion-sickness prevention, hoping their sons would sleep the entire time. It seemed to work; in fact, my nephews were unusually subdued when they climbed aboard my boat with their mountain of duffel bags and boxes of supplies. Addison, the two-year-old, was so drowsy that he didn't have the energy to fight his mother about donning his life jacket. He didn't attempt to tune my radar, and I didn't have to pull him away from the throttle and gearshift—not even once. Even Aubrey was so sleepy that he forgot to stand at the rail with my gaff, stabbing at every lobster buoy we steamed by. Thus we never had to turn around to retrieve a gaff jerked from his hands once he had succeeded in connecting with a buoy. There was a noticeable absence of squirming altogether. It was a quiet and quick boat ride to the island and an uneventful transit from dock to house. Then the boys emerged from their stupor just as the old folks were thinking about bed.

Oh yes, they woke up. And how! As I washed the dinner dishes, I was tickled to see my nephews wound up tight with excitement about being "on the Island." Little Addison ran around the living room, jumped on the couch, tripped over the dog, and went headfirst into a coffee table. The blow to his noggin didn't faze him in the least. He couldn't get into things fast enough— four flashlights, a deck of playing cards, a decorative glass ball, a bag of pretzels, the TV remote, a stack of CDs. He "fixed" my handheld VHF radio and "organized" some paperwork I had foolishly left within his uncanny range. He zipped from one thing to another, back and forth like a housefly caught and darting between windowpane and screen, then he happened upon a Tootsie Pop and stopped dead in his tracks. The sudden lack of turbulence grabbed his father's attention, and Charlie swooped down on the orange lollipop, yanking it from Addison's anxious tongue like a raptor on a rat. "No candy, Addison. It's bedtime." Wow. That was a mistake. Now little Addison had a mini tantrum followed by a massive and tearful outburst of begging and pleading for the return of his orange sucker. He was really unhappy, and his behavior brought to mind the phrase we coined especially for such outbursts: Addi—tude. His father was relentless and unyielding, and neither parent seemed bothered in the least by the hysteria. Although I understand that it would not be considered good parenting, I'd have given him the candy to restore peace. I noted with interest the source of the tears. It was not the lump now bulging from his head, but his intense desire for the Tootsie Pop. He was a Greenlaw, for sure.

All through the crying jag, his older brother, Aubrey, sat quietly with his father working intently with paper and crayons, creating a card for his mother, Jen. Jen was working diligently to try to put my house back together behind her wrecking-ball son. My boyfriend, Simon, who was on the Island for the weekend too, pulled a guitar out from under the sofa and began picking and strumming a familiar tune. Apparently music does have "charms," as Addison the savage let out one last whimper and slowly and shyly approached Simon.

Simon smiled and continued to play softly while Addison stared at the guitar and tapped his foot to the beat. When the song ended, Addison climbed up and sat beside Simon, the large man and guitar dwarfing my littlest nephew. Addison held his arms out, indicating that he would like the guitar in his lap, and said, "My turn." I managed to stop Simon before he was able to hand his coveted Martin to my anxious nephew. With visions of broken strings and sticky fingerprints, I bolted up the stairs to my bedroom and returned with a dusty, long-neglected mountain dulcimer for Addison to destroy.

"Here you go, Addy. Your very own guitar. Now you and Simon can play together. Won't that be fun?"

As I placed the instrument in his lap, Addison scowled as if to say, "You call this a guitar? Give me a break!" Addison threw the dulcimer onto the cushion beside him, insulted. He looked up at Simon, pointed at the Martin, and said, "I want that one." Now it was Jen's turn to spare the guitar, and she did so by announcing that it was bedtime. The brothers let out huge, audible sighs. Lower lips pouted, and the pleading for just a few more minutes began.

Aubrey handed his mother the card he had made with his dad's help and took a sudden interest in music. (Anything to avoid going to bed.) He joined his younger brother and Simon on the couch and reached for the discarded dulcimer. "No. Mine," Addison barked as he snatched the instrument back into his own lap. Aubrey knew that a fight would land him in bed quicker than a nice, quiet time, so he did not persist. Addison, poised with dulcimer, turned to Simon and said something that neither Simon nor I understood. Addison repeated it. It was two syllables, and began with *r*, but we could not decipher what he was trying to communicate. Aubrey, in his usual role of translator, informed us that his younger brother was saying "railroad," as in "I've been working on," and that this was Addison's favorite song.

Simon was pleased that he knew the chords and was enthusiastic about granting this request. Addison strummed the dulcimer in time with Simon, not in any particular key and with all strings open. The dulcimer proved to be a good choice for Addison, who strummed harder when the "fe fi fiddle-ee-I-oooo" part came along; since the instrument is inherently quiet, he couldn't make too much of a racket. I was glad I didn't own a set of drums or a trumpet by the time we sang "railroad" for the fifth or sixth round at Addison's repeated and insistent, "Again!" Over and over, Simon played as we all sang. This went on for at least an hour. I was so happy that my house was no longer being demolished, I just kept singing.

All of the adults were hoarse and sleepy from what was now beginning to sound like a satanic chant. It was getting late. I was getting ready to head upstairs. Even Simon, who is the nicest and most patient man, was getting a bit bored and attempted to play something closer to a lullaby, but the kids were like rock stars jazzed up on some stimulant. Finally, I couldn't take any more. I simply announced that I had to get up early to haul lobster traps, and was heading directly to bed. The adults were relieved and quick to agree that the time had come for all good little boys to turn in. Simon put away the guitar. And Charlie cut his sons off in midprotest, insisting that *everyone* was going to bed. "But

Mom didn't read her card we made her yet," was Aubrey's last stand. Jen stood and read aloud the poem Aubrey had written and decorated with pictures of trees and boats and stick figures.

> *I'm a little Indian on the go.*
> *Here's my arrow, here's my bow.*
> *When I go hunting, hear me shout,*
> *Bear and buffalo better watch out!*
> *I'm a little Indian with a fishing pole.*
> *A bucket of mackerel is my goal.*
> *I can cast to the middle of the bay.*
> *I want to go fishing every day!*

"Oh, thank you, Aub. That is lovely. Now if you plan to go fishing tomorrow with your father, you had better get tucked in right now." Jen's tone allowed no room for even one more second of procrastination. (I was, strangely enough, glad to hear that the Indian theme had not grown old with the kids. I remembered seeing notes that Charlie had left for "My two little Indians" signed "Chief Daddy Bestfriend.") There was quite a bit of commotion after this, which I took as the appropriate responses to what I understood to be an ultimatum: No bed, no fishing. The boys scurried around with hugs and kisses for everyone, buzzing now in anticipation of the day of fishing that they had been promised and which was always the highlight of a trip to the Island. This excitement, I might add, is something that Greenlaws never outgrow. I was sure that my brother would have as much fun as his sons.

It was a short night. When I heard two little voices downstairs, I glanced at my alarm clock. Five A.M. Cock-a-doodle-doo, I thought, and couldn't help but giggle as I heard the nephews barge into the bedroom where their parents were not too happy about the blond heads peering at them from the foot of the bed.

"Daddy, it's time to go fishing," I heard Aubrey state quite clearly.

"It's too early, Aub. Go back to bed."

"But you said 'early.'"

"Not *this* early. This is *too* early."

"Why?"

"The fish are still sleeping." Ah, there it was. The sun hadn't peeked over the horizon yet, and the first lie had been told. The fishing day had officially begun. There was not the slightest chance that the kids would actually go back to bed, or even leave their folks' bedside. So Charlie and Jen reluctantly crawled out from under the covers and began the breakfast routine. I had been looking forward to this since the last time they'd stayed at my place, when I'd first realized that feeding young kids is a lot like fishing. Charlie and Jen offered and prepared everything imaginable in an attempt to get Addison to "take the bait," but sometimes "they just aren't biting." My enjoyment came from seeing my brother and sister-in-law practice, in essence, my profession.

"Addison, want some cereal?"

"No."

"No, thank you? Want some eggs?"

"No."

"No, thank you? Pancakes?"

"No."

"You have to eat breakfast. Look at Aubrey. He's eating his cereal like a good boy. How about a nice bowl of cereal?"

"No."

"No, thank you? Well, there will be no fishing until you eat."

Although Charlie didn't yet realize it, I suspected, and Addison knew intuitively, this was lie number two. The cereal was soggy, the eggs were cold, the pancakes had been fed to the dog, and the toast was untouched as the fishermen began gearing up for the day. The brand-new Scooby-Doo tackle box came out of a duffel bag and the boys were fascinated with all of its tiny compartments and assortment of goodies. My brother patiently answered every "What's this?" and explained in detail the name and intended function of every doodad in the plastic box.

There were hooks and jigs and Christmas tree rigs and lures and sinkers and bobbers and spoons and rubber worms and poppers—the boys were absolutely mesmerized and getting increasingly excited and anxious to get out of the house. Charlie now assembled two small fishing poles with closed reels and stressed the importance of proper preparation for successful fishing. He told the boys that this "work" had to be done in order to enjoy the rest of the day. He taught them how to handle the rigs and discussed strategy and decisions that would need to be made. Where would they begin fishing? Would they fish from shore, or off the dock? Would they take the skiff? Would they troll, drift, jig, or anchor up and chum? What would they use for bait? By bringing the boys into the decision process, Charlie was making them take responsibility for the success or failure of the fishing, and I thought this was a good lesson for the boys even at their young ages. They would spend the rest of their lives making decisions about strategy in their everyday lives, and could definitely benefit from learning about the importance of preparedness.

While Charlie conducted the inventory-and-assembly process, Jen stuffed some extra clothes for the boys into a canvas bag and prepared a picnic lunch that looked to me to be entirely too healthy for a fishing trip. "Jesus, Jenny," I couldn't help but re-mark. "Whole wheat bread, cheese, carrots, apples . . . where are the Table Talk Pies and Hershey's bars?" This comment proved unwise, and was not appreciated by either parent when Addison began right where he had stopped the night before, pleading for candy. He was told that he couldn't have any candy because he had not eaten any breakfast. Tears were shed. This was my cue to leave, and I did so, explaining that I couldn't wait to hear all about their adventures at the dinner table that evening.

The fishing party was not far behind me. As I climbed into my truck, they marched with rubber boots and fishing poles out the front door and into the yard. (I couldn't help but notice a lol-lipop stick protruding from a very happy mouth.) Jen looked as though she'd been released from prison as she waved good-bye from the door and made Charlie promise to force the boys to eat lunch "no matter what," and to have a wonderful day. (Have a *long,* wonderful day was implied.) Charlie, standing in the weeds in front of my house, placed a surveyor's compass dangling from a loop of string around the neck of his oldest and began explain-ing how to use it. Here began the teaching of a most valuable life skill—navigation. I had been taught the basics of navigation as a young girl, and had grown proficient in the art under Alden's su-pervision.

As the fishermen disappeared into the woods with Aubrey leading and "keeping the needle on the big *N,*" I imagined what a magical day they would have. I spent most of my day aboard my boat wondering where they were, what they were learning, and, of course, what they were catching. I played many scenarios in my head starring the two boys.

That night at dinner, when they replayed their big day in

great detail, I remembered how much of an impression my early education in navigation had had on me. I saw a reflection of myself in Aubrey, who was infatuated with the compass and proudly wore it at dinner, explaining to me its function. Navigation, in its most basic form, is a skill that many never master. Aubrey, in one day, had already learned most of what he would need to know about it.

The shortest distance between two points is a straight line. We spend our lives as goal-oriented creatures, navigating from point A to point B, often encountering obstacles, which we must go through, over, under, or around. In this first lesson for my nephews, the goal was to get to a small, rocky stretch of beach due north of my house. In order to reach the beach, the fishing party would have to travel through the woods and bushes, over boulders, under blown-down trees, and around a wet swamp. As each obstacle was successfully overcome, Aubrey would get a bead on the "big *N*" and get back on course with his little brother close behind and his father bringing up the rear. Whether fishing from a boat or the shore, it's important to know how to navigate with a compass. There are obviously many easy analogies having to do with metaphoric compasses in our personal, professional, emotional, and spiritual lives. And we all can relate to encountering obstacles and "staying the course." What better way to teach young people about striving to achieve goals than giving them a compass and the responsibility for choosing their path as they tramp through the woods toward a fishing hole?

Leadership is something that I believe cannot be taught. People are either leaders or followers, and will learn which by trying out the different roles. This morning, Aubrey had been handed the compass, and as the older brother, would try his legs in the position of leader. I imagined him instructing Addison to follow close behind, or cautioning him of some danger and courteously holding a branch that might otherwise spring back, whacking his brother in the face. I had a hard time imagining Addison in the following position, but realized that at two years of age, he wouldn't have the attention span to learn how to use a compass. It's a long, hard trek for the little guys, and Charlie refused to carry Addison regardless of the "Please, Daddy," teaching him a bit about perseverance in spite of Addison's reluctance to absorb the lesson.

Another lesson that would be learned before the day was old was the importance of being a good steward of the natural world. Addison, of course, dropped his lollipop stick the minute he had chewed the last grain of sugar from it. Charlie insisted that he pick it up or they wouldn't be going one step farther. Respect for the environment has a lot to do with personal integrity. Gone are the days of raping and pillaging resources and the environment. The attitude of "Hey, no one saved me any buffalo" as justification for being environmentally irresponsible just doesn't cut it anymore. The age of two is a great place to start, and Charlie gave both boys the litterbug lecture, and off they went, a soggy lollipop stick in Addison's hip pocket as a symbol of conscientiousness and respect for his surroundings. (Again, I am in favor of fishing regulations; I just don't like stupid ones.)

By all dinner-table accounts, it had been a classic fishing day. Problem solving was tackled early with the need to figure out how to untangle lines and straighten bird-nested reels. Aubrey had graduated to fishing with a hook this year, while Addison flung a small, dull lead weight around wildly. He managed to bop his brother on the head a few times, but at least there was no danger of anyone losing an eye. A lesson in emergency response was taught when Addison slipped off a seaweed-covered ledge and into water. His father quickly plucked him out, explaining the reason for life jackets, extra clothes, and minding his father's words to "not go over there."

The fishing was pathetic, necessitating many moves in location and changes in gear. The boys learned about persistence and creativity. If you aren't catching fish, change something. Keep trying, and *never* give up. Finally, just about the time when the boys were thinking they would like to go play in their pirate fort, Aubrey's pole bent and straightened dramatically. Aubrey was reeling the line in as fast as he could and screamed, "I got one!" His father convinced him that he had only had a strike, and that the fish was not on his hook, as the line coming in was now limp.

"Cast it right back out there, Aub. You'll know when you have one. There's no mistaking that feeling of being hooked up." Aubrey did as he was told, was immediately hooked up, and nearly jumped out of his skin while cranking in the fish as it dashed back and forth just under the surface. When the fish was near enough, Aubrey, following his dad's instructions, lifted the end of his pole to pull the line and fish close so that Charlie could hand-line the fish onto the ledges where they now stood. The fish was pulled lip first from the ocean, and it dangled for a fraction of a second while the boys marveled at it; then it jerked itself free, plopping back into the water, where it vanished as if it had never been.

They fished and fished and fished with no luck, not even a nibble. The memory of the thrill of the tugging of the pole in his small hands kept Aubrey interested. The sight of that blue-and-silver mackerel flashing in the air for that split second kept Addison throwing his lead sinker every which way; occasionally he plunked it into the water. The three moved, regrouped, rerigged, and basically tried every trinket in the Scooby-Doo tackle box and every method in my brother's imagination and experience before finding the right combination. When they found it, the fish seemed to be in a feeding frenzy. Mackerel, big horse mackerel, were coming ashore hookety hook, as they say. Charlie could barely keep up with the releasing and untangling. Addison was so excited, he believed he was catching fish too.

Finally, the three realized they had just enough time to come home through the woods before dark. Two of the larger fish had been kept in the boys' lunch box for their dinner, while the rest had been allowed to swim free for another day. "We only keep what we'll eat," Charlie had told the protesting boys each time he tossed a fish back.

Now, at dinner, it was clear that Aubrey and Addison had been sworn to secrecy about the reason for their success. They had taken some sort of oath, and specific information was less than forthcoming. This tickled me, and I was intent on getting more details out of my nephews. I pried. I tried to trick them into sharing their location. I repeatedly asked about bait and gear, to no avail. They were so happy and excited and proud . . . and their lips were sealed. They were fishermen. All I was able to pull from Aubrey about their technique, other than the catching of "tons of fish," was his description of their method as "shock and awe." They were now, in their minds, part of this exclusive club that Alden and their aunt Linny (me) belong to. And they were ravenously hungry. As Jen set a plate of their now-grilled fish in front of each son, Aubrey referred to the dish as "whole wheat mackerel." Charlie tried to kick Aub under the table, but it was too late. Jen now knew what had become of the sandwiches she had made, the very same sandwiches Charlie had promised would be eaten by the kids. And I now knew the secret bait that led to such a successful day of fishing. I asked Jen if she might be willing to make me a couple thousand of those sandwiches for my next swordfishing trip, which got me a raised eyebrow.

Bedtime came. I wandered upstairs and climbed under the blankets and listened to the commotion still in full swing below me. The boys were wild, and Charlie was apologizing to Jen for not feeding them at all during the day. I wondered how many rounds of "railroad" would be sung before the little Indians would give in to sleep. Their education surely had not tired the boys as much as it had their father.

As I finished the tale of my nephews and tucked into yet another glass of wine at the Dry Dock, I realized that the tone of our conversation had softened and I was no longer irritated by Alden's remarks implying that he was the only *real* fisherman among the small gathering. True to form, he did comment that my brother was hardly one to coach his sons about life, as he was only thirty-five years old. "I should take those boys with me for a summer," Alden announced. "I've trained many a man aboard my boats," he boasted, "and they have all done very well." I remembered now that Alden frequently referred to his boats as "training vessels" and usually added that as soon as he trained a man to a point where he was worth having aboard, the well-trained man would take his new skills and find employment elsewhere. Nice, I thought, how Alden is convinced that his influence, even if very brief, has the power to take young folks from the bait barrel to the captain's chair, and can cite a number of examples of this phenomenon. I, on the other hand, could think of many times when things did not work out that nicely.

BAR SNACK

SEA SLANG

While thumbing through *Sea Slang of the Twentieth Century,* a book of old British sea slang, I was astounded by the number of entries for drink, drinking, and being drunk. It would appear that the Royal Navy was well into their cups much of the time. Sailors received an official issue of navy rum, referred to as a "tot." All sailors wishing to receive this "grog" before dinner each day did so. Sailors who did not "draw" their daily ration were called "temperance men" and were paid an additional three pence a day in lieu of their rum allowance. It's nice to know that we fishermen come by our eagerness to belly up to the bar quite naturally. Contemporary terms for drinking to excess include "getting caught in a rum squall" and "getting hung down on Commercial Street."

I know many sober fishermen, but it's more fun to talk about the ones who are not. What follows, though, is a list of classic and modern mariner lingo, a lexicon of sorts. It's worth mentioning that rum still is the first choice of liquor among my fishing friends. And the age-old question persists and remains unanswered: What *do* you do with a drunken sailor?

1. Toot: To drink in an impressive way. "Exercise toot" refers to a mild session, while "operation toot" is a spectacular binge.
2. Bleed the monkey: To steal grog from the cask.
3. Bung up and bilge free: The proper stowage position of a rum cask aboard ship.
4. Deep-sea tot: A short measure of daily rum allowance caused by the unfortunate roll of the ship.
5. Just awash: State of being hungover.
6. Carrying three red lights: To be very drunk. (A vessel displaying three red lights is a vessel restricted in her ability to maneuver.)
7. Splice the main-brace: To issue a double tot of rum in celebration of some occasion.
8. Walk the chalk: To prove sobriety.
9. Sun over foreyard: The approved time for drinking.
10. Let's call it eight bells!: Justify a drink prior to the conventional time.

COMPASS ERROR

The Dry Dock had begun to fill back up with people. I glanced at the handsome brass ship's clock over my shoulder and was surprised to see that it was after 5:00 P.M. It certainly had turned into a long lunch, which was not all that unusual. I had learned years ago, when I worked for Alden, of his habits at noon. If we were working aboard the boat at the dock and broke for lunch, that was the end of the working day. We usually worked straight through the lunch hour, as Alden knew too well that once that first rum and Coke went down, we might stay until last call. I excused myself from the table, admitting that I was heading to the pay phone to call my mother. I had planned to drive to Stonington and scoot across to the Island in time to join my folks at their place for dinner, but that was now out of the question, as I was well into my fourth glass of wine.

When I returned to the table, George and Tommy had pulled up chairs and were threatening to leave the bar for their boats. Surely their crews waited patiently for the captains to call it a night and head for the fishing grounds. I knew the two had consumed plenty of booze by this point, although they carried it well. They had probably built up quite a tolerance. In fact, George often complained of having "the Irish curse," the inability to get drunk no matter how much you drink. Younger fishermen boast of this malady, but at George's age, it was a complaint, as it made the effort to get shitfaced both time-consuming and costly. My chair was the empty one between theirs, and as I sat down, I felt slight in stature in comparison to the two hulks.

In my opinion, neither George nor Tommy has any real lust for commercial fishing, unlike Alden. They seemed to have sort of landed in the profession, and lacked whatever was needed to make a change. The most important thing I had learned from my friend was from my observations of the way he approached his life's work, not from his lecturing or advice. Working at something you love is truly fulfilling, and success can't be measured in dollars and cents. Now around the table sat examples from both ends of the success spectrum.

Some people are able to correct what Alden would call "compass error," while others simply live with it. Over the long haul, even just 2 degrees of uncorrected error will put you way off course. It's a basic fact of navigation and life. The longer the error goes uncorrected, the less likely it ever will be. Someday Tommy and George might wake up and have the courage to adjust their compasses, but it would take quite a drastic event, I thought. I wondered if they were now too far afield ever to find their way to their true destinations. Pondering this notion of waking up miserable one day and realizing that you are in the wrong life, and having the strength and wisdom to actually do something about it, brought to mind an acquaintance of mine. As soon as there was a lull in the conversation, I offered this story as food for thought for the misfit captains. Perhaps they would find the inspiration to pursue happiness rather than remaining stuck, square pegs in round holes. After a brief introduction, I began the tale of Brad.

In 1979, Brad Kraai (pronounced "cry") was going nowhere. He had graduated from high school the year before, backed out of going to college because he "wasn't ready," and was employed in a casket factory. Brad's hometown, a small one in a part of western Michigan that liked to call itself "the tulip capital of the world," was full of people of Dutch ancestry like himself. His best friend, Craig, was 100 percent Dutch too, and like Brad was blond and fair-skinned, although other than coloring, they did not look alike. Craig had an athletic build, while Brad had the boyish physique of one who can eat everything, and does, without gaining weight. They were both members of close-knit families and a community that valued hard, honest work. Like most nineteen-year-old men, these two buddies enjoyed drinking a few beers after work and discussing what they should be doing as opposed to what they *were* doing. "I think I'll join the Coast Guard," Craig announced after the last sip of his first draft one night. That seemed a worthy ambition, Brad agreed. And, with no more thought or consideration than that, the two found themselves in Grand Rapids signing up and taking oaths.

The only airplane Brad had ever been on in all of his nineteen years was the jet that flew him and his best friend to Cape

May, New Jersey, where they would endure the U.S. Coast Guard's brand of basic training. Craig had won the Navy League Award and was the top recruit in the company. Brad was less than gung-ho but found boot camp tolerable enough; mostly push-ups and head games. The two men successfully ignored the standard military-protocol bullshit that is part and parcel of basic training, and dreamed of being stationed on the Great Lakes, maybe even at Howland Station, close to home and away from this unpleasant weather and what had become known as "Cape May Crud," the relentless cough many developed from exposure to the area's unique mix of humidity and salt air. In the final days of the six-week program, it was announced by one of their instructors that there were ten open billets aboard the *Eagle*. Brad and Craig decided they would enthusiastically go after two of the ten openings.

When they received confirmation of the much-sought-after appointments, the men considered themselves incredibly fortunate. Their proud parents came all the way from Michigan to attend their graduation from boot camp and drove them to Baltimore, where they, and eight of their classmates, would join the *Eagle*, which was currently at a shipyard for refitting, maintenance, and preparations for "Summer Cruise." These ten seamen recruits had suddenly become seamen apprentices. It was very exciting. This year's cruise was rumored to be going to the Caribbean. Not bad duty for a couple of guys from small-town Michigan who, until now, had hardly traveled out of their home state.

The *Eagle*, a three-masted bark, was built in Germany in 1936 and initially served as a training ship for the German navy. Confiscated by the United States following World War II, the sailing ship became a training vessel for the U.S. Coast Guard, accommodating up to 170 of the academy's cadets on required cruises. Over 200 feet in length and with nearly 1,800 meters of sail surface, the *Eagle* is an awesome vessel and, as Brad and Craig and eight others quickly learned, a bear to maintain to the highest standards set by the Coast Guard.

Brad, Craig, and their parents were awestruck at the first sight of the beautiful tall white ship proudly bearing the red slash worn by all vessels of the U.S. Coast Guard. The *Eagle* wore an air of nobility in the shipyard among the countless other lesser vessels, and Brad felt important waving good-bye to his folks from her bowsprit. Brad and the others had been warned of the length and breadth of the work required on this billet, but the chance to go to sea as enlisted men among cadets (Daddy's little rich boys in the minds of those who had "come up through the haws pipe"), on a summer cruise stopping in many ports exotic to the guys from Michigan, would make it worthwhile. You have to think of it as a three-class system. The elite group was the cadets, the privileged academy students who were being trained as officers of the Coast Guard. Next came the professional seamen who actually ran the ship. Finally, there were the ten seamen-in-training who hoped one day to take their place as rank-and-file members of the Coast Guard. Still, no one aboard the ship considered themselves luckier than Brad, Craig, and the eight other trainees. The *Eagle* had led tall-ship parades. The *Eagle* had led sailing races. The *Eagle* had led many a Coast Guard cadet and seaman to a life at sea.

The *Eagle* was in the yard to have her main deck replaced. Before this could happen, she had to be stripped bare. The ten seamen, fresh from boot camp, tore into the work. They lived right aboard, enabling them to put in long hours. And with the scope of the project, long hours were imperative. They took down over five miles of running rigging, mostly manila line of large diameter. They dismantled countless blocks and assorted pieces of tackle. After they had decommissioned the rigging, the masts came down, all three of them: the foremast, the mainmast, and the mizzen. Yardarms were overhauled. The ten seamen assisted the union yard workers wherever possible, doing mostly dirty jobs that required no real talent other than a strong back and a tolerance for grime.

About a month into the project, the only real excitement to break the monotony was a fire aloft. Molten slag from an acetylene torch found its way into some chaffing gear around a radar bracket, smoldered, then burst into flames. There was a lot of scrambling around and yelling, but no proper organization. Although the end result was only a toasted radar, the scene was chaotic enough to dissuade some of the apprentices from staying with this billet. Six of them packed their sea bags and headed for other duties, claiming the fire was a "sign of things to come." Brad and the other three who remained, his friend Craig and two others named Richard and Kenny, figured their classmates were just not up to the harsh work, and found renewed enthusiasm in sticking it out. Richard was a bear of a young man, friendly but built like the guy you don't want to tackle. And Kenny was a real comedian and fun to have around. The four became fast friends. When the *Eagle* was put into the yard's dry dock, the four comrades were placed in a hotel where they pierced each other's earlobes using a sail needle. This somehow made them tougher, a more cohesive unit, more seaworthy. Because piercings were against Coast Guard regulations, the men wore Band-Aids, which detracted somewhat from the image they were after. So they found one of Baltimore's darker alleys and got themselves some bad tattoos.

With the massive amount of cutting and burning and welding being done by the union yard workers, and in light of the scorched radar, the young seamen spent days on end on "fire watch" and cleanup. Hanging around armed with water cans and attempting to tidy up what now looked like a disaster area was less than glamorous, but the four seamen stayed the course with the reward of a possible Caribbean cruise the "carrot on the end of the stick." (They were constantly told that they had to earn their right to make this trip by demonstrating their capacity for work; it was not by any means a sure thing that they would be allowed to go.) They drank a little beer at night and raised a little hell, as nineteen-year-olds will do, but mostly they were just exhausted from the work and didn't have enough energy to get into any real trouble in Baltimore.

Once the teak had been removed and the steel deck cut out, the ballast was exposed. One of the higher-ups determined that it should be cleaned. This would be a good job for the four seamen. The 300,000 pounds of steel cakes had not been touched in nearly fifty years, so this was a purely military exercise intended to test the boys and also ensure that they remained too tired to have any fun in the city. It was a long winter. The two boys from Michigan and the two others spent the bulk of it covered with grime and smoke from all of the cutting and welding. All the while, the thought of sailing this magnificent ship to the Caribbean was what kept them going.

Spring came and the summer cruise was looking questionable. The *Eagle*'s refitting was behind schedule. The teak that was to cover the new steel deck had yet to arrive, and some of the standing rigging had failed tension testing, requiring replacement. So there was increased pressure to complete the job: The Coast

Guard Academy cadets needed training cruises. Some corners were cut. The new deck was covered with nonskid rather than teak. The masts went up with a mixture of rigging, old and new. Brad, Craig, Richard, and Kenny worked feverishly, cutting, splicing, putting in thimbles and shackles. Richard's strength came in handy. Kenny's constant joking kept them all in good spirits. Finally, the announcement was made that the cruise would take place as planned and that the four seamen would be aboard. (It was common knowledge that the enlisted men actually ran and sailed the ship, while the cadets attended classes and learned how to use sextants and other obsolete instruments.)

When they left the yard in Baltimore and headed home to the academy in New London, Connecticut, much of the running rigging was still on deck. So, rather than sail, they steamed under the power of "Elmer," the *Eagle's* antiquated 12-cylinder diesel engine. Under way for the first time, even though not sailing, the seamen felt great. They stood watches and enjoyed a sense of pride and true accomplishment. They put the final touches on the *Eagle* in New London while the cadets were finishing the standard school year and getting excited about their cruise. The four seamen were constantly busy, stitching sails by hand and completing other tasks under the watchful eyes of many higher-ups. The ship was back to her original splendor and the seamen were very much a part of it. A three-day shakedown cruise was the highlight of their Coast Guard experience to date. Under sail, the men felt they had been born to go to sea. They studied diagrams at night and traced lines from belaying pins to sails during the day. They memorized the names, positions, and purposes of the 250 lines. They were sailors and they knew their ship. Hell, they had even cleaned the ballast! They had developed a true sailor's sense of entitlement and ownership.

They sailed brilliantly back to New London to collect the anxious cadets. The *Eagle* would be put back in her usual berth with the help of Elmer and with a very young ensign at her helm—an academy graduate of the previous year. The four seamen took their positions to throw heaving lines ashore. Brad thought they approached the pier a bit fast, but what did he know? He was just a lowly apprentice. Elmer hiccupped and stalled. Crash! The *Eagle* hit the dock so hard that Brad nearly fell to his knees. The commercial fishermen on the adjacent dock laughed and clapped their calloused hands. The engineers managed to get Elmer fired back up, but as the ensign pulled away to try again, the bowsprit caught a telephone pole on the end of the dock and brought it down with a clatter and another round of applause from the appreciative audience. The seamen, although embarrassed, were secretly glad that it had not been an enlisted man who had caused the commotion. The mistake was owned by one of the academy's star pupils. So much for the value of the chalkboard over the actual experience, Brad thought. The boat finally sidled up safely to the pilings, and once the lines were secure, the seamen quickly grabbed paintbrushes to fix the boo-boos. The training cruise should prove to be interesting, Brad thought as he masked the scratches with fresh paint. He would certainly enjoy the dynamics of the joining of these two different worlds—the academy and the "school of hard knocks." Yes, it would be quite an education.

A few red faces and a quart of paint saw the minimal damage disappear and the *Eagle* was officially ready for the summer cruise. Exactly 125 wide-eyed students of the academy boarded their new home with the same feeling of awe for the ship that the four enlisted seamen apprentices had initially felt, that feeling now replaced with pride and confidence. The first port would be Boston, Massachusetts, and the timing couldn't have been better. Beantown was celebrating her three hundredth birthday and OPSAIL 80, perhaps the biggest maritime event in history, was on the *Eagle*'s dance card. The *Eagle* would lead tall ships and sailing and other historical war vessels from around the globe in the grandest of saltwater parades. This was truly a big deal, and the four comrades couldn't have been more excited. The hard times during the months in the shipyard faded away like labor pains.

Brad's parents traveled to Boston to visit their son. Five festive days were enjoyed without a hitch (other than a liquored-up Brad getting lost in the city, on a bicycle, and delivered back to the ship by a sympathetic Boston cop). The icing on the cake was the start of the cross-Atlantic race of the tall ships. Although the *Eagle* was heading ultimately to the Caribbean, she began the race with the others. Twenty-four hours after her bowsprit crossed the starting line, the *Eagle* was 40 miles ahead of the field. With an air of "no competition here," she made a hard starboard turn and got about her business of making sailors of cadets on their summer-training cruise.

Sea time under sail; the men were euphoric as miles of saltwater passed under the *Eagle*'s keel. While the cadets attended classes and learned the science, theory, history, and mechanics of what they were living, the four apprentice seamen were getting their hands-on training from the enlisted men who ran the ship. They learned, among other things, how to "step the masts" to allow the *Eagle* passage under low bridges. Brad was a natural, and quickly became the foreman, taking the job of directing the hydraulic operator and pulling the masts' pins when stepping was necessary. This required that Brad work 50 feet above the deck, and he became comfortable and at ease in the rigging. The education the four seamen gained from this and their multitude of experiences was worth more than any tuition could buy.

They hadn't sighted land for days when Bermuda appeared and disappeared on the horizon. Bermuda! The boys from Michigan couldn't believe it. The tiny island in the distance could have been another planet. They had seen Bermuda!

When they crossed the Tropic of Cancer, the virgins (those who crossed for the first time) partook in the usual rituals. The Tropic of Cancer is one of three imaginary lines that circle the earth horizontally. Cancer, at 23½ degrees north latitude, runs right through the Bahamas, and the boys were so excited about their progress they minded neither wearing their underwear over their trousers nor kissing King Neptune's belly. (Neptune was not available, so a fat electronics technician substituted.) The Bahamas! They had passed the Bahamas! The apprentice seamen could barely hide their excitement from the cadets, most of whom had visited both Bermuda and the Bahamas on family vacations. They contained themselves for fear of appearing uncool. Soon they would be in the Caribbean. It was like a dream.

The first stop in the Caribbean was Puerto Rico, where no one was allowed shore leave. This was disappointing, but Brad and his buddies made up for it in the Virgin Islands. As enlisted men, the four apprentices were free to come and go from ship to shore, unlike the students, who were kept on quite a short leash, standing watches while the seamen played. Brad and his three shipmates took a ferry over to St. Croix, where they swam, snorkeled, lay in the sun, and drank rum and coconut milk. Now the four men felt quite privileged. They prayed that this cruise would never end. To think that this was considered work.

The next port of call was St. Lucia, down the chain of Windward Islands. They enjoyed perfect sailing conditions, and Brad and his buddies spent days aloft, looking around and down at the water that was truly as blue as they had heard it would be. They were mesmerized by acres of porpoise that rode the ship's bow wake and seemed to follow behind and alongside like faithful dogs, man's best friend. They saw birds they had never heard of before and loved every second of their newfound paradise. The *Eagle*'s crew threw a beach party on St. Lucia and even some of the officers let their hair down. Life just couldn't get any better. Brad pinched himself every morning and laughed as he recalled that just a few short months before, he had been working a dead-end job at a casket factory.

The men hated the idea of leaving St. Lucia, but the lure of Barbados promised more fun. So, with Barbados as the next stop, the men readied the ship for departure from St. Lucia. With no tugboat available to help turn the *Eagle* around and head her in the right direction out of the tiny bay, someone gave the orders to use a mooring buoy off her stern to assist with the maneuver. This resulted in one of the more dramatic mishaps of the training cruise. A hawser (that's a large-diameter line) was run to the mooring buoy and around a windlass on the stern of the ship. The windlass (anchor winch) was manually driven. Ten cadets marched around in a circle pushing on 8-foot lengths of 4-by-4 timber. They marched and pushed and strained and slowly cranked the ass end of the ship off the dock and toward the mouth of the bay one click at a time. Soon the huge mooring buoy was underwater. What a lesson in physics! The hawser was singing tight, and the cadets continued to march slowly around. Click, click, click . . . just a bit more and they would be able to swing right around and sail off into the horizon. Bang! The ratchet mechanism of the ancient windlass gave way and timber and cadets flew like berries in a blender. (Picture a child's toy airplane driven by an elastic band. Wind it up tight, and let it go.) The scene scared everyone into silence. Fortunately, the worst of the injuries were minor broken bones. Another lesson in physics. Once everyone had recovered from the shock, and the bones had been attended to, the *Eagle* was once again under way. The consensus was: That is why we call this a "training cruise." Things happen aboard a ship. Handling bad situations is part of the training.

That mantra soon became the excuse for everything that went wrong. It was all part of the training experience. Well, nothing went wrong in Barbados. In fact, everything was perfect. The windlass episode was soon forgotten, and a week of beaches and R&R was appreciated by the cadets and enlisted men alike. Barbados was the most beautiful place Brad had ever been. Sadly, they had to leave it. But Santo Domingo was next on the schedule! It would be a long sail to get there, with plenty of training, but Santo Domingo was reputed to be lovely. So, they sailed and trained and looked forward to the next stop in the next paradise. Brad and his shipmates ran the paint shop, stood watches, and did a variety of things while the cadets attended classes and learned in class what the enlisted men had been taught in basic training and while putting in their time in the shipyard.

A slight mishap during "small-boat exercise" resulted in an impromptu man-overboard drill, and the cadets who were left treading water while the ship got back to rescue them chalked their swim up to training.

Santo Domingo was hot and impoverished. The days and nights spent there were uneventful, probably due to the fact that the training cruise was winding down, and the men were winding down too. Some of the *Eagle's* crew traded with the locals through portholes as the ship departed for Miami. *Playboy* magazines and sandwiches were exchanged for handmade coral jewelry. This cruise was coming to an end. The four young enlisted seamen were anxious to get home and put in for new and exciting billets. Now that they had traveled and seen so much, Brad and Craig were ready to find duties on smaller Coast Guard vessels closer to home.

After a brief stop in Miami, the *Eagle* pulled into Charleston, South Carolina, where there is a huge Coast Guard presence. Charleston proved a bit of a homecoming, and celebration was the order of the day. Brad and company partied with "Coasties" from several other vessels, drinking beer and sharing exaggerated stories of seagoing exploits. At 1:00 A.M., the seamen found themselves in a local bar where Brad became infatuated with a girl. He thought she was pretty neat, and was doing his best to flirt when he was rudely interrupted. The man who butted in was making rude comments about the object of Brad's attention, and Brad, being the gentleman and brave, experienced sailor that he now was, asked the man to step outside. The man was more than willing to oblige. A typical brawl ensued on the sidewalk, including a sucker punch thrown by one of the man's friends. The unexpected blow sent Brad reeling into a parked car. As he leaned over the hood of the vehicle, he wondered where his buddies were. He could certainly have used some backup. When Craig, Richard, and Kenny finally squeezed through the ring of spectators, it was not to enter the fight, but to drag a dazed comrade back to the ship.

They walked. Brad's head began to clear. It sank in that he

had left the bar without the girl but with what felt like a broken jaw. In disgust, he kicked something. It turned out to be a brick. Now he limped aboard the *Eagle*. Within a few hours, his friends decided they needed to take him to the navy hospital back on shore. After he was admitted, Brad watched his pals leave to catch the ship that would soon be heading back to the academy. "Don't worry," they assured him. "We'll fill in for you until you get back aboard." Brad wondered where they had been when he was getting his jaw broken, but thanked them and promised to catch up with them in New London. Some training cruise this had turned out to be.

Bright and early the next morning a navy doctor operated on Brad's shattered jaw and fit him with a kind of rigging of his own, designed to keep his face stable while the bones healed. Brad closed his eyes and bowed his head, waiting. The light that had warmed his face and now shined on the crown of his blond head felt like a ray of sunshine, and he easily imagined what was now being slipped over his head and around his neck to be a lei placed by the petite, tanned hands of the most beautiful Hawaiian woman. This delightful image was jerked away by the brusque tone of the doctor's voice. "You'll need these snips to cut the wires if you feel the urge to throw up. Otherwise you may choke and drown to death in your own vomit." The thought was nearly self-fulfilling. Brad swallowed hard, looked down at the scissors that were to dangle on his chest while his jaw healed, a medallion signifying youthful stupidity, and gallantry for naught.

The military hospital did not have the luxury of a full administrative staff, so the infirm were expected to perform whatever duties they were capable of until discharged. Brad was given the job of manning the admissions desk. Greeting people and answering phones through a mouth wired shut? Brad thought it a cruel joke and considered it part of his punishment. The worst part, of course, was that his ship had departed without him to complete the final leg of this training cruise. Brad hobbled down a corridor on a broken toe and a cast that ended at midcalf. Why had he chosen a *masonry* brick to kick? A man in a fresh uniform with walking papers sarcastically offered Brad a piece of chewing gum as he passed. Disgusted, Brad squashed a bug with the heel of his cast just because he could, then felt bad about doing so. His jaw ached. This was a disgrace. He sat at the desk and willed the phone silent during his shift. Some training cruise it had turned out to be. Oh, he had learned plenty. But probably not what the Coast Guard had intended.

The phone rang. Brad, feeling quite in the dumps about himself, realized that he was on the wrong end of this act. He was no ventriloquist; he was indeed the dummy. This thought made him smile, and he winced in pain. He reached for the phone and the dueling aches in jaw and toe reminded him again of why he was here. After some mumbling, he finally managed a muffled greeting. Much to Brad's surprise, it was his mother on the phone. She was nearly hysterical. All he could understand was her repeated "It could have been you." All the while Brad was thinking that it *had* been him. What was she saying? When his father's voice came through the receiver, everything was clear. His friend and shipmate Richard had been killed while performing Brad's duties in stepping the mast, ". . . squashed like a bug." Strong Richard, dead. Brad felt something rising in his throat, and he reached for the scissors that hung around his neck.

● ● ●

Alden, George, and Tommy were all silent. I didn't know if they were thinking about Richard, about friends they had lost at sea, or about close calls they themselves had had. I explained how my friend Brad was now happily employed off the water. It took the death of a friend to show him that the Coast Guard, in fact any life at sea, was not for him. He had learned that it's never too late to correct your course. I looked at George and Tommy. "Not everyone is cut out for life at sea," I added, just in case they had missed the point.

"Yeah," Tommy said. "Like my friend Gus. Man, talk about someone not fit for the sea. He ignored all the signs for the longest time. Talk about compass error . . . he was off about one hundred and eighty degrees." Tommy was either thicker skinned than anyone thought, or maybe clever to switch the focus away from himself. Alden caught my eye and grinned. He had not missed my intention to jab George and Tommy. George, aware of Alden's alliance with me, urged Tommy to tell the story of his friend Gus and managed to keep their own lives' compasses out of the spotlight through the next round of drinks.

BAR SNACK

THE BIG ONE THAT GOT AWAY

The most prominent theory when it comes to fishing gear, both commercial and recreational, is that it's best to use the lightest tackle possible for a job, as "shy gear" will enable the fisherman more hookups. Lines are rated according to three separate criteria: their breaking strength, stretch, and diameter; which of these is most important depends on personal preference and the intended application. Any sport fisherman worth his salt can recite world-record catches by species, weight, and gear class used. Unfortunately, the tendency toward favoring shy gear results in a higher percentage of lost (prematurely released) fish, and more and greater stories of "the one that got away."

• • •

Jeff Waxman was taking a "busman's holiday" and loving every minute of marlin fishing off Cape Hatteras. Before dawn on the third morning of his weeklong trip, Jeff stepped aboard Dr. Kelly Gibbs's 28-foot sportfisherman with great anticipation and the usual excitement big-game anglers feel when getting geared up for a day on the water. Just two days earlier, this same team had boated a 546-pound blue marlin, so they were pumped up for a repeat performance.

At 9:00 A.M., four lines rigged with ballyhoo came off reels. The captain suggested a "big bait" for the "long rigger," and Jeff obliged with an 18-inch swimming mullet sporting a 2-ounce chin weight. As Jeff dropped the mullet back into their wake, a huge, dark, submarine-shaped shadow appeared immediately beneath it. The monster fish inhaled the bait greedily, much to the delight of the fishermen. Jeff enthusiastically set the hook. This was almost too easy, he thought as he settled into the fighting chair's harness. The mate quickly cranked up the four slack lines and, once everything was cleared and stowed, Jeff leaned back, putting a bit of pressure on the fish. "She came out of the water up to her shoulders and shook her head. She was huge! We were speechless." The men guessed this blue to be 1,400 pounds. A 1,400-pound blue marlin on a 50-pound-class Penn International reel—this feat would clearly earn a world's record, and would require patience, finesse, and physical endurance. Three hours passed with the fish putting Jeff through some paces; alternately "greyhounding and sulking," she easily pulled him off the seat of the chair. When he felt several quick bumps against the line, Jeff feared sharks were attacking his trophy, and the captain backed the boat down hard while Jeff spooled the slack as fast as he could. Now close enough to see her under the surface, the men were astounded. Their prize wasn't being eaten; she was feeding in a school of 20-pound blackfin tuna. She swallowed the tuna like kernels of popcorn. She gulped down six while the men stood, dumbfounded. "It was as if she had no hook in her mouth."

After the marlin had sated her hunger, she settled into a steady northwest trek. Six hours after the hookup, Jeff's excitement had diminished, along with his energy. His feet were bleeding in his boots and his shoulders and thighs were blistered with sunburn. The reel's drag was nearly as fried as Jeff's legs, so the decision was made to put a move on the tormenting fish. "No more Mr. Nice Guy. We had to take her."

Another three hours of sheer torture ensued. The angler got the line up as far as the wire leader *forty-seven* times! The mate grabbed the wire and had it torn from his hands each one of those forty-seven times, and was now as exhausted as Jeff. Nine hours of fighting and finessing and backing the boat down, and they were 21 miles from the hookup. "It was like a modern-day Nantucket sleigh ride." The men agreed that they hadn't much left in the way of strength, and decided to make one last attempt. The captain would back down hard and fast, the mate would take a double wrap around his raw hands, and Jeff would man the flying gaff hoping for one Hail Mary shot.

It seemed the fish sensed the imminent flying gaff. "She went crazy!" The fish shot up like a rocket from a launch pad, shook her stubborn head, snapped the wire leader, and belly-flopped, drenching the spent fishermen. This would-be world-record-setting blue marlin would take her place among the grandest of "the ones that got away," and this story and other tales like it raise the question of which end of the line is doing the fishing. Nine hours, 21 miles, a 250-pound man, and 50-pound-class tackle? The marlin may have bragging rights.

9

BACKING AND FILLING

As Tommy floundered around, trying to get his story started, he explained some things to us about his friend Gus. By the time he finally began weaving the tale, I was convinced that the story was somewhat autobiographical, and not about Gus at all. He painted Gus as a man in a chronic state of indecision, uncomfortable in his own skin, and although diligent in work, dithering in life in general. "Backing and filling" is old sea slang for the motion of the sails of a ship when she is "in irons" and unable to make headway. I wondered out loud if Gus was simply backing and filling, searching for his niche and trying out different roles for fit. "Nah," said Tommy. "He's just got a short attention span. And he's wicked indecisive."

• • •

Gus's problems all started with, "Get off! If you can't do a better job than that, get off. Go home. I don't need you." Gus felt like dying, but being the son of the captain (not just *any* captain), he did not show it. He grabbed his suitcase, which appeared to have been packed by an extreme anal-retentive, and made his way topside under his father's seething stare. Neatness was more than an admirable quality aboard; it was ship's law. Everything, including personal items, had to be kept "Bristol fashion" (shipshape) per order of the captain. Gus—a strikingly handsome young man with a rare combination of thick, dark hair and blue eyes that held the ocean's reflection even when landlocked—and suitcase hit the dock in Secretary, Maryland, in 98 degrees and humidity and began the 8-mile walk to the closest Trailways station for the next bus home. During the long walk in the heat, his only thoughts were of getting there. But once aboard the bus, the bit of cool air mixed with diesel fumes reminded him of the ship, and what had gotten him fired . . . yet again.

Staring out the window and catching glimpses of the Choptank River and specks of the Chesapeake Bay through the passing foliage, Gus wondered whether it had been the brass nameplate, or the bank of batteries, or both that had been responsible for the hasty termination of his employment this time. Had he forgotten to polish the brass plate on top of the valve cover of his father's Gray Marine diesel engine? Or, God forbid, perhaps he had neglected polishing the batteries. Gus's father, like his father before him, demanded that his Chesapeake Bay freighters be maintained like beautiful women, "clean, pristine, painted, varnished, shined, waterlines like lipstick on a lady." Any time at the dock waiting a turn to take on a load of oyster shells was spent keeping each workboat (75 to 100 feet in length and overpowered) gleaming like the sleekest of yachts. Excessive, Gus thought, but he was raised to work like a bull, not question orders, and even to polish batteries.

Gus flung open the kitchen door and led his entrance with the suitcase. His mother, Becky, who was the only one home, took one glance at the suitcase and knew immediately what had transpired. She wiped her hands on her tidy white apron, and with that unique balance—that only a woman could ever manage—between compassion and love of son/mate, and understanding and appreciation of husband/captain, she asked only if her son was hungry. The answer of course was yes, although Gus hadn't thought of food all day.

The meal was calming and his mother nurturing until she mentioned that Gus's uncle Albert was actively looking to hire another mate for work on his tugboat. "No," was all Gus could muster in response. He imagined the only thing worse than working for his father would be to ship out with Uncle Albert. One-armed Captain Uncle Albert was, in Gus's opinion, a bigger slave driver than his father had ever dreamed of being. And it was widely understood in the business that Uncle Albert was a bit insane. His father might be a perfectionist and a maniacal workaholic, but Uncle Albert was all of that and, in addition, just plain mean. Uncle Albert ran a tug, *The Fort Comfort,* for the McCarren Marine Contracting Company, based out of Norfolk, Virginia. Hundreds of mates had come and gone under and out of the horrid man's rule. The thought of leaving home for Virginia to work on *The Fort Comfort* with the dreaded one-armed uncle was out of the question.

Fired on Thursday, up and out of bed at 3:00 A.M. the following Monday with the same suitcase, packed with obsessive attention to orderliness and with clothes newly cleaned by his mother, Gus stood at the end of the driveway waiting to be picked up by Uncle Albert. Much to his own surprise, he had taken the job. After all, he had been out of work for three whole days. Like any decent and self-respecting seaman, Gus used this waiting period to take stock of his life and contemplate the perpetual questions of "how" and "why."

The only thing Gus knew for certain was that he had been born with a disdain for laziness. His family's sole measure of human worth was work. Anyone who did not work, and work hard, was a no-good bum. Productivity was life's number one priority, ranking ahead of both health and happiness. A stint with the legendary uncle was probably in order to pay penance for whatever he had neglected while under his father's command. Gus had come by his obsession with diligence quite naturally, he thought as he pondered his lot and present situation, suitcase in hand at the end of the driveway.

Gus's grandfather "Pop" was born in Reedfield, Virginia. At the age of six, he was orphaned and adopted by the Caleb Jones family of Smith Island, Maryland. In the 1920s, it was not unusual for a family to adopt a young boy to become part of their workforce and thus contribute to the family's bank account. In Pop's case, the Jones family made no secret of this. Gus remembered his grandfather saying the only reason the Joneses had adopted him was "to make a slave of me." And it seemed they did. At the tender age of six, Pop was working on an oyster dredge boat in the cold dead of winter and a crab-scraping canoe in the heat of summer, which converted him from tender at six to tough at seven. Work was synonymous with survival in those days, and Pop worked like a dog. Doing the work of a grown man

during childhood tends to hasten the maturation process. At sixteen, Pop and his new bride (Smith Island born and bred Lillian)
sailed into Crisfield, Maryland, aboard his crabbing canoe to start
a new life. He built the canoe himself as a means of escape. They
never returned to the island.

They worked, and their offspring worked, and they prospered.
A Chesapeake Bay Skipjack replaced the canoe. Then another
Skipjack was acquired, and another. And then powerboats . . .
until Pop had a fleet of workboats and captains and crews. Gus's
grandfather built two marine railway yards so that he could maintain, service, and repair his own fleet. Gus's father returned home
from World War II to join his father in the marine railway and
workboat business. Business boomed and was carried on the
backs of these men and, eventually, forty-five other employees.
The work was strenuous "bull work" and consisted largely of
manhandling big, heavy timbers and planks. An honest day's
work was demanded of all employees, who were compensated
with sixty cents ($.60) per long hour. Backbreaking labor was of
the utmost importance; money was secondary. The value was in
the means, not in the ends. The harder they worked, the more
valuable their existence. If you did not work, you did not deserve
to breathe. Gus, pondering this, took a deep breath as headlights
came quickly around the corner and lit up his face.

At 4:00 A.M. sharp, Gus threw his suitcase in the back of the
company station wagon and climbed in with Uncle Albert, his son
Jake, and the mate Walter. Walter was a Native American, and
was introduced as Indian Walter. (Gus later learned that Walter
was wanted by the law in several states and figured that was why
he never heard his family name.) The ride to Norfolk was quiet.
Uncle Albert drove, Jake and Indian Walter slept, and Gus fretted

about his new employment. As Indian Walter snored with his mouth wide open, Gus couldn't help but notice the absence of teeth. Three hours later, they found the end of the ride, which did nothing to boost Gus's low spirits. The station wagon pulled through a construction-yard gate and crept slowly in the early light to the dock where the tug, *The Fort Comfort,* was berthed.

A loud, obnoxious blast of the car's horn startled Jake and Indian Walter into wakefulness. Like infantrymen responding to a bugle, Jake and Indian Walter were instantly alert. Doors were flung open, duffel bags were grabbed, and the men jumped aboard the waiting tug. Gus followed Indian Walter to the forepeak. Walter opened a hatch-type door, pointed at the bottom bunk, and said, "You, there." Gus placed his suitcase in the bunk as Indian Walter muttered something about a "candy ass" and hurried toward the engine room. Gus followed, hoping to be given some orders. He watched as Indian Walter checked oil and water levels and cranked up the 12-cylinder GM diesel engine that powered the tug. No sooner had the engine started than another horn blared. This time it was *The Fort Comfort*'s air horn, and one-armed Captain Uncle Albert leaned on it way too long. This was clearly the signal to cast off the lines, and Walter nearly barreled Gus over getting to the bow. Jake was in position at the stern line, so Gus hustled to handle the spring lines. Gus knew how to handle lines; he'd done it all his life. He could do it with his eyes closed, but that didn't keep the captain from barking commands. Uncle Albert seemed to be the type who made unnecessary and excessive noise so that everyone else understood that he was indeed doing something.

A week passed, and Gus was unhappy. The work was hard, and that was comforting. But this was not the site for him. His sixty-one-year-old uncle was always rushing and trying to prove to the company's superintendent that he was the best captain in the fleet, at the expense of his crew. In terms of marine propulsion, Uncle Albert was all cavitation, constantly spinning his wheels with excessive noise and little to show in the way of progress. He sure stirred things up, though. This was obvious to Gus, who had been raised working alongside men who were all traction, methodical and wasting no motion.

Uncle Albert had an abnormal hatred for anything built by General Motors, so he occupied himself with trying to destroy the tug's engine by going from full ahead to full reverse whenever possible. This irritated Gus, who had been taught to treat the machinery like a lady, gently and with finesse. His uncle's rough treatment of the tug was just one more manifestation of Albert's deranged mentality, Gus thought. As soon as another job opportunity presented itself, Gus would be gone.

In the second week of his employment on *The Fort Comfort,* Gus realized that he had fallen in love with the area of Hampton Roads. The Roads consist of the James, Elizabeth, Pagan, and Nansemond rivers. The perpetual motion of ships and tugs throughout this complex waterway fascinated Gus and he studied the tides and currents at each bend and learned quickly. The tugboats were designed for pushing, pulling, or carrying heavy loads. They were slow to respond to a course change or a decision to stop, which made the job quite exciting. But given his lack of confidence in Captain Hookless, situations that should have been exciting were simply nerve-racking. Tragedy lurked around every corner, and the ever-conscientious Gus found it impossible to relax. He loved where he was, but hated who he was there with. He hoped for a change.

Bunking with Indian Walter was the worst part of this miserable experience. Walter's hobby was making knives. He would lie awake at night filing and shaping pieces of scrap metal into exotic replicas of old weapons such as pirate swords and other assorted cutlery. Every hour Indian Walter spent honing metal into lethal weaponry was an hour that Gus lay awake sweating. If Walter wasn't sharpening a blade, he was cleaning his gun. He kept the 22-caliber revolver in his pocket at all times, which seemed to make him happy and Gus even more uneasy. Gus wanted desperately to quit and go home, but couldn't bear to disappoint his folks, who he was sure must think of him as quite a failure, unable to keep a job. Gus knew that he could never wait out Indian Walter. Walter was held captive on the tug, a slave to Uncle Albert. A fast-moving and busy tug was the perfect hiding place for a man on the lam. Uncle Albert had Indian Walter by the balls. The two men had clearly been born centuries after their time. They would have been famous pirates. Gus prayed for a change. A few nights later, his prayers were answered.

While playing with his revolver, Indian Walter came up with an idea to play Russian roulette with one bullet, and Gus. After a couple of shaky, terrifying rounds, the air horn interrupted the game before anyone actually blew his brains out. The tug nudged the dock, and Gus and his forever-faithful suitcase hit the ground running. "Hey! Where do you think you're going?" screamed Old One-Arm. Gus turned to see Indian Walter's toothless grin and never answered and never again looked back. Finding himself once again at a bus station with the same neatly packed suitcase, Gus dreaded the ride home from Norfolk. As much as he was infatuated with the waters of the area, he had to go home to find another job.

The very next day, sitting in his parents' kitchen, Gus scanned the pages of *Boats and Harbors News Journal*. And there it was. On page 32, under the employment section, was an ad that Gus figured had been placed by God himself. Gus read the ad four times.

WANTED

100-ton captain for sightseeing vessel.
Chesapeake Bay, Hampton Roads waters.
Only single-screw experience need apply.

Call ASAP.

Gus couldn't dial the phone fast enough. The very next day, the bus carried Gus and suitcase back to Virginia. Standing nervously in the Newport News Harbor Cruise office, Gus looked out at the world's largest harbor and knew this was where he belonged. He felt at home for the first time in his life, and a wave of confidence that he would land the job came over him. Gus met with the owners of the business, whom he liked immediately. They all shook hands and Gus had the job. He was elated.

Captain Gus proudly took command of the *Kicotan Clipper*. She had been converted from a Chesapeake Bay buy boat, exactly like those of his father and grandfather that Gus was so familiar with. She had a shallow draft to accommodate shoal oyster beds, 65 feet of length, 20 feet of beam, and a single engine. The pilothouse had been lifted in the conversion to sightseeing vessel to allow for a second deck, room for more customers. And she was pretty. Beautifully maintained, the *Kicotan Clipper*'s waterline was like "lipstick on a lady." As Gus met the other captains, he learned that his boat was the least-coveted vessel of the fleet due to her design, single screw (one engine, one shaft, one propeller—as opposed to twin screw), a conversion that had rendered the *Kicotan Clipper* difficult to steer and control. She was heavy topside, which caused her to "roll the yeast out of the biscuits." No matter; Gus was young and tough and happy to call the boat his. And, he was gainfully employed again.

Gus quickly learned the routine. Each of the well-maintained vessels owned by the Newport News Cruise Company carried 150 passengers and ran five tours a day—at 10:00 A.M., noon, 2:00, 4:00, and 6:00 P.M.—seven days a week. The tour consisted of the Newport News Shipyard, the small boat harbor, the Norfolk Naval Base, Hampton Harbor, Craney Island, the James River Bridge, and past hundreds of boats, barges, ships, and tugs. It was a waterman's field day, a mariner's candy store.

Gus was a natural. He knew the ebbing and flooding tides out of the James River, and respected them. He knew when to cut the tour off and race back to the dock to load the next group of tourists. The mates were young, courteous, and well trained. The *Kicotan Clipper* was hard to steer, and she would list drastically with a wind or course change or shift of passenger load. She was, Gus thought, a bit unstable. Still, his anticipation was excellent, and he quickly got used to her. Gus ran the tours every day for two months. His folks should be proud, he thought. He had been bred to work, and work he did. He felt good about himself and his new home. He thought he could do this forever. But "the two o'clock" on the last Tuesday of July changed all of that.

Flat-ass calm and 100 percent humidity multiplied the heat of the day to that of a broiler. The air in the harbor was sickening. Smoke and exhaust from the ships and dust from the coal piers hung in the atmosphere like grease on the walls over a Fry Baby. This was the classic "weather breeder" of which all mariners are wary. The first two tours went smoothly, without a hitch, as usual. The Roads was at its peak season for boating activity. Tugs moved ships, pleasure boaters zipped around trying to stir a breath of air, sailboats drifted aimlessly, fishing parties dangled hooks over the sides of head boats, and Gus and his crew loaded another 150 perspiring vacationers onboard the *Kicotan Clipper.* Before casting off the lines, Gus took time to listen to the weather radio. Chance of storms here and there, this and that, maybe, maybe not; because the forecast was so iffy, Gus was uneasy. There were dark clouds looming to the northwest, but there were two busloads of eager tourists. What would the other captains think if he were to cancel a trip? What would the boss think? Was it all about money? Yes, Gus knew the Wartons had many paychecks to sign. But in Gus's mind, it was all about expectations and appearances. He was expected to run the tour, and he didn't want to look foolish or chicken or disappoint anyone. Against Gus's better judgment, with a blast of the horn the *Kicotan Clipper* slipped away from the pier.

Outside the harbor, Gus turned to port and headed up the James River for a tour of Newport News Shipyard. As the dark mass to his northwest grew nearer, Gus upped the throttle a bit, turned to port, and headed toward Norfolk to show the customers the naval base. The weather was turning sour, but the Coast Guard had said nothing, so it probably looked worse than it was. Appearances again, Gus thought. Just in case, as he passed Middle Ground Lighthouse, Gus ran at an angle to the strongly flooding tide to save time while still allowing the tourists to see something. He had to give them their money's worth. Gus knew the value of a hard-earned dollar. Abeam of a field of aircraft carriers, Gus turned to port to head back to Norfolk just as the radio announced a "severe weather warning to mariners."

The warning was right on target. Gus could see "a ten-mile-wide wall of hell" charging the James River and bearing down on the *Kicotan Clipper*. Running at full throttle and sailing with the enormous tidal current, Gus thought he could make it to homeport before being engulfed in the storm that was clearly raging just above the bridge. When the office called to check on his progress, Gus explained that he was racing Mother Nature back to the dock and that everything was under control. Seconds later, the view of the James River Bridge disappeared in the heart of the squall and Gus's heart sank. The speed of the storm's approach was surprisingly fast. The *Kicotan Clipper* could not withstand the intensity of this system. Gus grabbed the radio's microphone and informed the office of a quick decision to "hide" from the storm, as he clearly did not have the ability to outrun or survive its wrath.

Gus remembered sea stories told by his father and grandfather about "hiding under a ship" in a tugboat in perilous weather. The idea was to sort of park the tug in the shadow of a bigger ship, on the ship's lee side, which would shelter the tug from the wind. At the time, they were just stories shared by salty old men. Now Gus wished he had paid more attention to the stories, or better yet, he wished those men were with him. But the young captain was on his own. The closest ship to his position was the *Mariner Star*, a coal carrier of 800 feet in length. She was massive, heavily laden with her load of coal, and soon to be the *Kicotan Clipper*'s best friend. Steering straight for the ship's stern quarter, Gus approached her slowly, making contact as gentle as a kiss. Gus held the *Clipper*'s bow against the black steel hull, increasing the throttle to maintain contact pressure as the wind increased. The passengers were frantic with wondering what was going on, and why the boat was not running for the dock and what they thought of as safety. They were afraid of the unknown; Gus was afraid of the known. Gus ordered his crew not to roll down the plastic rain windows for fear that the additional area would give the wind more surface to grab and result in the *Clipper* rolling beyond a point from which she could recover. Soon the rain was pelting down and the passengers scurried for cover, listing the boat severely.

The brunt of the storm held 85 to 100 knots of wind. Gus was now at three-fourths throttle to keep enough pressure on the ship's hull to remain in her lee. The wind was beating against the *Kicotan Clipper*'s windows, causing them to vibrate loudly and eerily. In the highest gusts, the boat would shudder and the passengers would shriek accordingly. Using the lighthouse off his port beam as his only reference, Gus became aware that the *Mariner Star* had begun to swing on her mooring. Now at full throttle, Gus feared that the big ship would soon come around with her bow into the wind and he would be blown off to fend for himself. There was no way they would survive. His odds had been better playing Russian roulette with Indian Walter. Gus's life was now unwinding before him and he questioned once again the "why." His family would be disgraced should one of their own be responsible for the end of all of these lives. He prayed, and vowed "never again"—should he somehow miraculously make it ashore alive.

It was a miracle, or at least the strength of Mother Nature, that may have saved the *Kicotan Clipper*. The force of the tide was enough to keep the big ship from swinging fully into the wind on her anchor. After what seemed like hours of torture, the wind subsided and the *Clipper* left the lee of the big ship to head for the dock. Gus was wiped out, totally drained physically and emotionally. The passengers exited quickly and silently. Gus looked at his suitcase and wondered what to do. The radio reported distress calls from mariners less fortunate. Lives were being taken. This day's "two o'clock" had taken its toll. Gus and his suitcase had made their final tour and they decisively departed the *Kicotan Clipper.* That was it for Gus and the sea. Today he works as hard as ever, selling golf carts.

When Tommy finished, Alden cleared his throat, ensuring he had our rapt attention. "Russian roulette is the point," said Alden. "Aren't we all spinning the chamber every time we leave the dock? Sometimes we gamble with our lives, and sometimes it's just money. But anyone who gets out of bed in the morning is playing the odds. Some of us are able to ignore that fact and enjoy our work, while others are constantly backing and filling." He ordered up another round of drinks. "I'd rather take the bullet at sea than sweat about my chances with a spin anywhere else."

BAR SNACK

RED RIGHT RETURNING

While browsing in a bookstore, I happened upon the nautical section and pulled from the shelf a book on sailing. Even though I've spent a ton of time at sea, almost none of it has been aboard a sailing vessel. As a result, I have only the vaguest idea of how to sail (as opposed to motor) a boat. Eager to learn, I opened the book and read, "You can't trim sails properly if you don't know which way the wind is blowing." Well, I thought, no shit. If you don't know which way the wind is blowing, perhaps you should stay home. Maybe I knew more than I thought I did. I skipped ahead a few chapters, landing in "Personal Safety," and found two full pages dedicated to "Staying Onboard," the opening sentence of which read, "The best way to avoid drowning is to not fall overboard." Again, I thought, No shit. And if you ignore this stellar advice and do fall in, the book recommended that you "get rid of objects with negative buoyancy, such as tools." So, the only thing I actually learned was that sailors are no smarter than fishermen.

One rule of thumb for beginner sailors, according to the above-mentioned book, is "When in doubt, let it out." I assume that has something to do with sails or the boom, but it brings to mind the fisherman's equivalent: "When in doubt, scream and shout. If you truly do not know, run in circles, go below."

We have hundreds of silly sayings, rhymes, acronyms, and little cheaters to nudge our memories for important concepts in navigation and seamanship, and to help us read the weather. The following is a list of the first ten that come to mind.

1. "Red Right Returning." This is widely understood to be a reminder to leave red navigational buoys to starboard when returning to a harbor from sea.
2. "Red over white, fishing at night." A fishing boat engaged in fishing at night is required to display an all-around red light over an all-around white light at the masthead.
3. "True Virgins Make Dull Companions At Weddings." This is a cheater for converting true course to the compass course. Each first letter stands for a step in the process (true, variation, magnetic, deviation, compass, add west).
4. "Can Dead Men Vote Twice?" This is the same thing in reverse, used to convert from compass to true (compass, deviation, magnetic, variation, true).
5. "Red at night, sailors delight." When the sky is red at

sunset, the next day should be beautiful according to this common saying.

6. "Mackerel skies and mares' tails make tall ships carry low sails." High, wispy cirrus clouds and rippling cirrocumulus are indicators of an approaching storm.

7. "When boat horns sound hollow, rain will surely follow." The atmospheric conditions and height of cloud cover, if any, affect the way the sound of a ship's horn travels and its tonal quality.

8. "Sound traveling far and wide a stormy day does like betide." Similar to number seven. This may suggest that you can hear bad weather approaching.

9. "When the glass falls low, prepare for a blow." When the barometric pressure drops, the wind will blow.

10. "Red over red, captain is dead." Two red lights vertically displayed in the masthead is the sign for a vessel not under command.

10

END FOR ENDING

It was getting late. We had stayed at the Dry Dock much longer than I had planned, and I still had not accomplished my mission. Every time I tried to bring up Alden's health or suggest to him that he might consider retiring or at least slowing down a bit, someone started telling a joke or a story that led to another and another . . . like rounds of drinks. I now noticed that Alden had switched to drinking coffee, and thought I might do the same. George and Tommy had swung around in their chairs to chat with a buddy across the room, leaving Alden and me in as private a situation as was possible. This might be my last chance this day to talk seriously with my friend, I thought. "What does your doctor say about caffeine?" I asked.

"It's decaf. And if I wanted my mother here, I would have invited her."

"You don't have to be so nasty about it. I'm concerned about your health, that's all. Would you please consider retiring from fishing? You might live longer."

"Live longer? To do what?" From his tone of voice and the drumming of his fingers on the tabletop, I realized I would have to shift gears. How could I discuss this in terms that wouldn't insult Alden or put him yet again on the defensive? He's right, I thought. What would Alden do in retirement mode? He has no hobbies. He has no interests outside of fishing. He used to enjoy flying his plane to spot fish, but he hasn't been able to pass the pilots' annual physical for years. I couldn't picture Alden taking up a musical instrument or art lessons or golf. The thought of Alden in Bermuda shorts made me laugh. Impatient, waiting for my response, he added, "If it takes me all day to get one lobster trap off the bottom, I'll be happy to spend my dying day doing just that."

Taking a different tack, I suggested that Alden continue to fish for a living, but perhaps consider missing a day in bad weather, or fishing half days so that he could get more rest. Alden didn't believe in vacations and seldom took a day off for even the major holidays. I suddenly recalled a phone conversation—it must have been at least five years ago—when I'd told Alden that I was taking a trip off from running the *Hannah Boden*. I remembered his response as clearly as if it had been this very day. "You *need* a trip off? That's a laugh. You haven't been around long enough to need end for ending." Maybe this would be the key, I thought. Maybe I would use Alden's own words to get through to him. "End for ending" is the term for flipping a line used in standing or running gear end for end to lessen the strain on certain sections and vulnerable parts. It helps to avoid parting off in heavy weather and is a way of spreading out the wear and tear to get more life out of line and gear, sort of like flipping a mattress. Before I could suggest the end-for-end technique in reference to his work habits, I thought perhaps I would get Alden to lower his guard by reminding him of my famous "trip off" story, which has become one of his favorites. I took a sip of wine, ordered a cup of coffee, and began the telling.

It was with trepidation that I left the *Hannah Boden* at the Pan American Dock in San Juan, Puerto Rico, and headed home to Maine for the only vacation I had taken since accepting the job as skipper four years earlier. In the world of commercial fishing, I was just beginning what we refer to as "a trip off," as in a month spent somewhere other than aboard the boat I was captaining. Fishermen rarely go on vacation, but do occasionally take a trip off or stay ashore while the vessel, crew, and transient captain head out as usual. In this particular case, it was the boat's owner, Bob Brown, who agreed to take the helm for this February's moon. I guess what I was most nervous about was the possibility that Bob and my crew would put a whopping trip of swordfish aboard and realize that I was indeed dispensable and quite re-placeable. What if they found that they could actually function without me? Well, I had convinced myself that I should eventu-ally find out, and now was as good a time as any.

I shivered all the way from touchdown in Boston to my folks' house. It actually felt good to have goose pimples and chattering teeth. My first week in the Caribbean, some three months before, I had thought I might die—perish from the heat. I cut sleeves and collars from every shirt in my sea bag and spared the legs of only one pair of jeans, which I now wore. My crew dubbed my new wardrobe "custom-cut Caribbean," as all alterations were a bit ragged due to the absence of scissors and presence only of a knife, or "ripper." Although there was no mirror in my stateroom, I imagined I looked pretty cool sporting one severed sleeve on my head to keep bangs out of face and bait out of hair. The makeshift scarves always matched my top, but the style never caught on. When I asked my cook's opinion of my fashion sense, his response was, "It's a good thing you can catch fish." I did acclimate eventually to the extreme heat; I even slept covered with a blanket after a while and regretted chopping up all of my clothes, the remains of which now entered my parents' home in a green garbage bag slung over my shoulder.

I received hugs from Mom and Dad and had just barely said hello when the telephone rang. My mother answered it, then handed it my way, whispering, "It's Bob Brown." I greeted my boss in the most pleasant manner, as I always did, and explained that I had just now come through the door. I imagined he must have a quick question as to where I might have stowed some tool he surely needed and could not locate. Boy, was I surprised to learn that he had fired my entire crew fifteen minutes after my departure and was having more trouble than he anticipated finding good men wandering around the dock. To say that Bob Brown wasn't the most popular guy around would be an understatement. Bob was desperate to get fishing by the first quarter of the moon, and insisted that I return to Puerto Rico pronto to work on deck for him. After all, he urged, working on deck would be easy—just like a trip off—without the mind-numbing concentration and smothering responsibility of running the operation. I conceded that point, and agreed to return the next morning, not confessing that I was secretly relieved that the trip would not go on without me. Even if I hadn't wanted to go, there would have been no point in arguing; Bob Brown was the model of persistence and determination, and always put a convincing spin on any plea. Those attributes endeared him to those who knew him well, and had the opposite effect on everyone else. So, back to the Caribbean I would go to work for the boss. Oh, and I was to bring a couple of men along to fill out the deck crew.

My friend Ivan, a great deckhand, readily agreed to make the trip. He was familiar with both the *Hannah Boden* and her owner through previous fishing experience, and his love of the vessel and desire for a dose of sunshine easily persuaded him to go to Puerto Rico. I hadn't seen Ivan in a while and was anxious to work on deck with the big, lanky guy with the mop of blond hair and perpetual smile. Good old James the Irishman was my next phone call. I found him at ABC Taxi in Portland, Maine, where he often hung out with fellow countrymen. James was game. The three of us met in Boston's Logan Airport the following day and boarded a direct flight to San Juan.

Working on deck with James and Ivan would be a treat, as they are both very competent seaman as well as good company. Relinquishing the reins to Bob Brown would make for a relaxing month at sea, or so I thought.

As Ivan, James, and I climbed into a steaming-hot cab in San Juan after an easy flight down, I wondered what position I would take on this trip. I had worked my way up through the ranks, so I knew I was capable of any job, be it cook, engineer, or whatever was needed, but I most enjoyed working on the fishing gear itself. I liked baiting hooks while setting out, and fine-tuning the gear while hauling back. Sharpening hooks and replacing chaffed or nicked monofilament leaders is great busy work and at the same time is imperative to the success of a trip. The work required of the gear boss becomes quite remote, leaving the mind free to wander to other, more exciting places, a luxury I had not enjoyed since becoming a captain. I might well spend the month daydreaming.

The cabbie drove through the gate of the chain-link-fenced Pan American Dock and by the guard shack from which Latin music streamed. As far as waterfront goes, this area was the worst—very industrial and quite filthy—making it easy to head to sea. Trash was littered along the hot tarmac and a pack of stray dogs scouted, probably looking to kill one of the rats I had seen. (The rats appeared much healthier than the dogs, I might add.) In a word, I would best describe that place as "infested." There lingered an odor unique to this dock: the smell of oil, diesel fuel, garbage, and sun-dried fish juice. At the dock itself, fishermen, longshoremen, and crew members of ragtag island-hopping freighters formed two lines at the only pay phones in the vicinity, smoking cigarettes and shuffling impatient feet while each waited his turn for AT&T.

Comparatively small, pristine longline vessels appeared through my open window as we approached the far end of the wharf. I pointed out the *Hannah Boden* to the driver and he stopped beside the pretty green boat just long enough to collect his fare and for us to jump out. There in the middle of the *Hannah Boden*'s deck stood the very square Bob Brown, hands on hips and shaking his head. "This is my crew? Is that the best you could do?" he yelled and laughed teasingly.

"I'll box his ears for him," muttered James under his breath, but loud enough for me to think that perhaps Bob and James might be like oil and water. We climbed aboard single file. Bob shook all hands. As we engaged in idle chitchat about the flight, up from the engine room emerged a hot, sweaty, and irritable Max Stoner. I had a hard time pretending to be happy to see Stoner. Ivan (who is far nicer and more polite than I) actually groaned. James had never had the Stoner experience, so it wasn't until later that he realized just how miserable life could be.

Stoner had worked for me aboard the *Hannah Boden* in the past, serving as engineer and "butcher" (fish cleaner). He was, hands down, the most negative person I had ever met, and working around him was a drag. And, he stunk—literally stunk. Everyone knows what it's like to be around a complainer, but it's magnified tenfold when aboard a boat, as it is nearly impossible to get away from the source. (This holds true of the odor problem too.) Stoner hated everything and everyone. I got so tired of his incessant grumbling on one trip that I ordered him back in the stern where he was to work on gear day in and day out, never showing his face forward until I escaped to the pilothouse. The "gear in the stern" was a two-man operation, which led to some problems. No one else wanted to spend time next to Stoner. So they developed a tag-team approach; the men took turns in the stern with Stoner, dreading every second of the unpleasantry. "Whose turn is it to work with Stoner?" elicited responses more appropriate to the question "Who wants to eat shit?" Stints in the stern with the grumbling Stoner grew shorter and shorter, until the deck of the *Hannah Boden* looked like it was host to a continuous game of musical chairs. When the men asked me to order Stoner to shower, I laughed. When they informed me that he had prepared the sandwich I had just inhaled, I nearly threw up. (And they laughed.) So, here I was about to work on deck with Max Stoner. Things couldn't have been worse.

Bob, or Brownie, as we affectionately called him, wasted no time putting his crew to work. First, we loaded the bait—ten thousand pounds of frozen squid. Stoner set himself up on the freezer end of the chain, which did a lot for his profuse perspiration problem. I, knowing how bad it could be, set myself up on the dock end, two full links away. Just as the last box was tucked into the bait freezer, the groceries appeared along with a fuel truck. Stoner trudged toward the engine room to man the boat's elaborate fuel-intake manifold, unhappy at best. "He's a right miserable fuck," James noted.

"Wait until we cast the lines off. It gets worse," Ivan added as we began to unpack and stow the three thousand dollars' worth of food that would satisfy us for the month at sea. Brownie's wife, Suzanne, had done the grocery shopping, and was to make the trip working as cook and photographer. I had been swordfishing for fifteen years at this point, and had never shipped with an official photographer. But, what the hell, I thought . . . as long as she did the cooking, I didn't care if she thought she was Steven Spielberg. It sucks to be the cook aboard a fishing boat. I had done it, and had absolutely no interest in going back.

Stoner entered the galley as I was putting cases of soft drinks into the walk-in refrigerator. He leaned over me, peering in at the stash and said, "What the fuck? Juice boxes? She must think we're fuckin' two-year-olds. Where the fuck's the Pepsi?" I agreed that perhaps Suzanne had made a small miscalculation when I too counted the cases of kiddie-size boxes of drinks complete with their own straws, and noted zero aluminum cans of soda pop. I shrugged my shoulders and smiled, unwilling to give Stoner the satisfaction of an ally. Staring into the refrigerator and marveling at the number of boxes of chocolate-flavored Yoo-hoo,

I began to wonder how this trip would play out. It would certainly be different.

By 8:00 P.M., the boat was fully supplied and ready for sea. Brownie announced that we would leave the dock at first light, so we had the evening to ourselves. Stoner made it known that he was headed up the street to the Black Angus, a whorehouse, as far as I knew, which is why I never eat beef in San Juan. When Ivan suggested that Stoner shower and change into clean clothes, Stoner was clearly disgusted and barked back, "What the fuck for?" And off he went with his money and intentions. To this day, I believe I may have seen Max Stoner grin.

Brownie and Suzanne got cleaned up and went out to dinner and a movie. James, Ivan, and I remained aboard the boat, stowing our personal gear and making up our bunks. I had my usual stateroom in the wheelhouse, intended for the captain, which I appreciated due to the fact that it came with a private head and shower. The Browns had moved into the starboard stateroom on the main deck level, James and Ivan would share the port stateroom with its two bunks across the companionway and just forward of the galley, and Stoner would have the "pit" with its four bunks and lockers all to himself. That was one certain advantage to being Stoner—privacy at bedtime.

We were all weary from the traveling and long day hustling to get the boat prepared for departure on schedule. (Swordfishing trips are kept in sync with the lunar cycle. It's very important to reach the fishing grounds by the first quarter. More moon equals more productive fishing.) Bob Brown was a stickler for keeping the *Hannah Boden* at sea and off the dock. I said, "Good night," and headed topside, knowing that when Bob said "early" he meant it. Just as I turned to leave the galley, Stoner stepped in from the deck. I said, "Good night, Max," which was not intended as an inquiry. In return I got a grunt. Ivan enthusiastically commented on the short time Stoner had been gone. Something to the effect of, "Jesus! *That* didn't take long!"

"Fuck you."

"Good night, Max Stoner. So nice to meet you. I am so looking forward to getting to know you better," James piped up sarcastically.

"Fuck you too."

Oh yes, I thought, this would indeed be an interesting trip. I lay awake in my bunk contemplating this diverse pool of humanity and wondered if I was as weird as each of them. In the end, I decided that I was not.

The biggest contrast was between Stoner and Ivan. Ivan is as pleasant and positive as Stoner is miserable. Ivan is fun to be around and as good a conversationalist as James, but clearly more playful and lighthearted than any of the rest of us are. Ivan is not only a voracious reader, but actually assumes the persona of the main character of whatever he is reading. (Hence the name Ivan, short for *Ivanhoe*, the book he was reading when I first met him.) His mannerisms, language, and even his posture are transformed when he is in the midst of a good read. Once we discovered this, the rest of us used him to test one another on how well read we were. The most frequently asked question aboard the boat when Ivan crewed was, "What's Ivan reading?" I thought I had detected a slight swagger this morning and clearly heard an "arrrrrr," so assumed Ivan was immersed in *Blackbeard, Terror of the Seas* or its equivalent. Actually, it was *Treasure Island*. Close. Regardless of his chosen charade and role playing at any given time, Ivan was a delightful companion at sea. Between Ivan and Stoner, the entire spectrum was covered.

True to form, Brownie stuck his head into my stateroom before sunrise with a joyful, "Cock-a-doodle-doo! Rise and shine! Breakfast is on the table!" I had forgotten how important meals were to Bob. He liked his victuals and referred to himself as "fat as a porpoise" although he really was not; more stocky, I would say. Well, I didn't like to miss any meals either, so was in the galley before the toast popped up. I joined the others at the table just as Stoner was lamenting two things: The first was that Bob had wakened him in the middle of the night to "vacuum under the refrigerator." Wow, I thought. Brownie must have had to crawl around on his belly to notice that. The second was that Bob had wakened him again to cook breakfast, as the cook was seasick. Wow, I thought. Seasick? We hadn't even left the dock yet. The thought of Stoner preparing this meal was enough to turn my stomach, but there was no beef included, so I managed to shovel down a plateful of breakfast while Ivan entertained us with his new pirate talk. When Ivan stood, I noticed the large knife in the handmade sheath that dangled from his belt. He reached across his body with his right hand, pulled the knife from his left hip, wielded it dramatically, and growled, "Arrrrrrr." Then he laughed like hell. Ivan's laugh is so infectious—a combination of a large man's chuckle and a boy's giggle—that I too began to laugh. Bob began to laugh. I even heard a chuckle come from Suzanne in sick bay. Stoner snarled, and James just looked at me and shook his head, as if to say, "What have you gotten me into this time?"

I wondered, in spite of my anxiety over the possibility of the gang having a successful trip without me, if perhaps I wouldn't have been better off staying ashore and risking the shattering of the illusion of my irreplaceability. For one fleeting second, when Brownie declared it time to cast off, I fantasized about jumping ship and flying back to Maine. When my mind returned to real time, I was on the bow of the *Hannah Boden* coiling a dock line to be stowed until we were back at this same pier many miles, days, and (we hoped) fish away. Brownie looked elated at the wheel, and Suzanne rallied to film our departure from San Juan Harbor. I thought it must have been quite some time since Bob had taken the boat himself. He seemed excited, almost to the point of being manic, I thought. Perhaps I had become too remote and had been taking these trips for granted. Brownie's enthusiasm might be contagious, I hoped. Perhaps this trip would put the fun and thrill back into the business for me. Or, it could have the opposite effect. I reminded myself of why I had asked for a trip off to begin with: I had felt a bit burnt out.

The first twelve hours of the steam to the fishing grounds were delightful. James, Ivan, and I worked in the stern of the boat, in the sun, on the "leaders" (part of the fishing gear), while Stoner assembled and tested "beeper buoys" (more fishing gear) and went about the various chores expected of someone in his position as engineer. He did so with a fair amount of griping. Suzanne had recovered fully from her bout of queasiness and prepared a marvelous dinner that we all enjoyed as the first quarter of the moon crept over the bow. The timing, as was usual with Bob Brown, couldn't have been better. In twenty-four hours, we would be making our first set. I realized how relaxed I was—carefree—nothing to worry about. My only responsibility was to keep the leaders in pristine condition and take a two-hour watch each night. Maybe I wasn't so burnt out after all.

When, later that night, Stoner shook me from a very deep and restful sleep, I bolted from my bunk to take responsibility for the ship and sleeping crew for my two hours of watch. I was getting my wits about me and realized that Stoner was agitated and had said something about the engine. I stepped from my stateroom into the wheelhouse and asked him to repeat what his problem was and he said, "The fuckin' engine sounds like it's coming unglued!" I now realized that it was not my watch, and that Stoner had wakened me to report a mechanical problem. I hustled to the console and pulled the throttle back to an idle and out of gear, shut the engine down with the push of a button, and advised Stoner to wake up the captain, as this was now his responsibility, not mine (thank God). Stoner voiced his apprehension about waking Bob, so I brushed by him to do it myself.

Brownie in the meantime had of course heard or felt the sudden lack of propulsion and was coming out of his stateroom before I could knock on the door to roust him. "What's the trouble?" Bob asked, tucking the tails of his blue shirt into the green work pants he called "the uniform." I explained what had transpired and that Stoner was certain that the main engine had some serious ailment. Stoner and I followed Brownie to the engine room and watched him pull and inspect the dipstick for the lube oil level. Satisfied with the level, and relieved that there was no sign of water in the base, Bob did a thorough visual inspection of belts and whatever else he thought might make a clatter such as Stoner had described. Finding nothing amiss, Bob proceeded to start the engine. Wow, what a racket! Bob quickly hit the kill switch and shut the engine down. The look on his face was both knowing and disturbed. Bob Brown had spent most of his life at sea, and was therefore no stranger to breakdowns. He had a great working knowledge of diesel engines and knew well how to turn a wrench. Bob Brown had never been on the receiving end of a towline.

We got to work under Brownie's guidance. As we drifted, we carefully disassembled the top portion of the main engine. The first quarter of the moon set and a full sun rose as parts were removed from the engine, gaskets scraped, and pieces cleaned and set aside in an organized fashion. When Brownie discovered a bent push rod, his hopes of fixing the engine and getting under way to the fishing grounds collapsed. Bob didn't know what had caused the rod to bend, but understood that running the engine in its present condition would be mechanical suicide. We needed to get back to San Juan to get parts and have a certified Caterpillar mechanic repair the damage. We needed a tow. But here is what happened: Not one single captain in the rest of the fleet would answer Bob Brown on the radio. Not one. That's how much they disliked him. So, it was impossible to ask anyone to drop everything to tow us ashore.

Brownie, who was well aware of most everyone's feelings about him, asked me to please try a few of my fishing buddies on the radio. Although I was able to get replies from the four captains I hailed, the answers were all the same, and it looked as if we might be adrift for quite some time. Everyone felt that if the roles had been reversed, and they needed a tow from us, Bob Brown surely would not have interrupted his fishing trip to help unless they were in imminent danger. We were drifting safely and were in no danger whatsoever, so they all felt we could, and should, just call for a commercial tow as anyone else would. It was implied and understood that Bob Brown was an extremely successful fisherman and businessman who could well afford to hire a tow. The fact that he was such a tightwad, went the logic, was no one's fault but his own. The rest of the fleet, I was convinced, was enjoying our predicament, and I could almost hear laughter over the speakers, along with the "It couldn't happen to a nicer guy." It was exactly what I had anticipated, but when I repeated the other captains' suggestion that Bob pay for a tow, my boss was not pleased.

Brownie, it soon became clear, was quite a scorekeeper when it came to favors he had extended and now rattled off a huge list of things that either he or one of his captains had done for other fishermen, going back as far as 1967. The longer the litany of tows, lent parts or gear, and good advice, the more indignant Bob became. Brownie figured he had a bushel basket of IOUs in receivables and was livid when he discovered, in this time of need, that they were uncollectible. Indignation grew to scorn, and scorn ignited some weird instinct for retaliation. I was absolutely forbidden, as his employee, to help anyone in any way ever again. In fact, I should not even speak to anyone on the radio.

"Who needs them? . . . Bunch of losers. None of them would make a pimple on a fisherman's ass. Pay for a tow? That will be the day! I'll show them." Then Bob went into some kind of a trance. He stared out the wheelhouse windows over the *Hannah Boden*'s bow and chewed sunburned skin from his lower lip. His black eyes became mere slits as he concentrated. "Call the Coast Guard! They'll tow us in. I'm a taxpayer!" I hoped that Bob did not intend to have me call the Coast Guard. "Call them now." Apparently he did. I do not recall which station answered me, but the gist was that if we were in no danger, the Coast Guard would not respond, and I was advised to call a commercial towing company in St. Croix for assistance.

"Tell them we're taking on water!"

"I will not tell them we are sinking! You're the captain this trip. You lie to the Coast Guard if you'd like." And I stretched the microphone's cord toward my anxious boss. I had never ignored an order given by a captain before, but now I made an exception.

Brownie squirmed a bit, unhappy that I would not be his mouthpiece. "Tell them that the main engine is down. That's the truth. Tell them that the generator sounds funny. I think it does. Tell them that we may lose all ability to pump the boat out, and should we begin to take on water, we will be in peril. Tell them we are just being cautious and attempting to avoid a potentially dangerous situation. Preventive measures . . . they like that sort of talk." I begrudgingly relayed all of this to the Coast Guard, and the next thing I knew, a helicopter was dropping a pump onto our deck. Brownie's scheme to get a free tow was foiled. Would he call for a commercial tow? Hell no. "I'll sail this rig back to San Juan!"

I assumed that Bob was overwrought with anger and frustration and would soon come to his senses and call St. Croix for a tow. But when he ordered me to gather the rest of the crew in the wheelhouse, I became skeptical about his ability to behave like a normal person. Brownie seemed almost triumphant when he declared that we would *sail* the *Hannah Boden* back to San Juan. I too like a challenge, but sailing a 100-foot steel vessel that was designed to be propelled by a large engine is more than a stretch. We were all silent (speechless) as Bob worked out the sail plan in his head. This was ludicrous, I thought, but said nothing. He's gone nuts, I thought. What would we possibly use for sails, our bedsheets? Bob must have read my mind, as he quickly announced that we had three blue tarpaulins aboard that would work quite nicely as sails. Now we all stood with our mouths open in amazement that he was indeed serious and determined to go through with the childish scheme. We would miss the entire moon. I wished I had insisted on taking this trip off.

The next thing I knew, Ivan was up in the mast stringing up the first of the three "sails" while the rest of us stood on the bow looking up at him. Brownie barked orders aloft and Ivan responded with a hearty "Aye-aye" to each command. There was not even a breath of wind, but Ivan seemed to be enjoying this exercise, as it fit so nicely into his pirate world. I have never heard so many "Shiver me timbers" and "Blow me downs"! Ivan called down to us cheerfully for some help, referring to us of course as "mateys." This looked like the only way we might get back to port, so we all pitched in with the rigging. I still can't believe that anyone thought to try sailing the *Hannah Boden*. Stoner disappeared to the engine room to disassemble more of the engine so that it would be ready for the mechanics whenever we might get to port.

Hours went by. We rigged and rerigged tarps from mast to outriggers, trying to understand what Brownie had in mind. Bob became a bit frustrated with his crew's lack of sailing experience and surmised that our painfully slow progress toward the dock might somehow be attributable to poor rigging rather than absence of wind. It was hot. We were getting weary of the constant climbing up and down, pulling on lines, tying and untying. No matter how we rigged them, the tarps hung limp. "He's daft as a brush! He's a raving lunatic! Next he'll ask us to row her ashore!" James had about had it with this charade. He went below and came back with a couple of ice-cold Yoo-hoos, offering one to me. We sat and sipped silently as Ivan continued happily to adjust the tarps. I finished my drink with a slurp through the straw and pitched the drink box over the side. Ivan was truly in his element. He stood perched in the crow's nest, hand shading his eyes from the sun. He looked and looked and looked, and I fully expected him to yell, "Land ho!" Still, the tarps hung limp. James asked if I was familiar with "The Rime of the Ancient Mariner," and I laughed.

We pretty much agreed to humor Brownie until he would eventually come to grips with the fact that we were not moving and that he would have to pay for a tow. We did as we were told and were apologetic about not being more knowledgeable sailors. I had never been aboard a sailboat of any size, so really did not understand the physics of the whole thing. When Ivan made some noise, we looked up to see him pointing off to the east. There was a raft of ripples creeping across the mirrorlike surface. "Wind!" Ivan repeated. This was quite exciting. As the breeze grew near, James and I were on our feet and ready to take orders. The tarps responded. At first they fluttered; then, as we tightened lines, they filled. The wind was not strong, but steady. Ivan and Brownie were happy with themselves, and James and I were relieved to hear, "We told you so," as it looked as though we might get ashore sometime. Brownie manned the wheel and Ivan stayed aloft, tweaking the tarps to maximize our speed. We sailed and sailed and sailed. It was fun. The sun was going down and, as the day cooled, the wind increased slightly. We sailed into the night and into the following morning. When Stoner came up from the engine room for a breath of air, he was irritated as usual. "This is fuckin' stupid. Can you believe this shit? Hey, when Jolly-Fuckin'-Roger comes down from his post, I could use some help in the engine room."

"Lighten up, Stoner. This will be over soon. We'll get the engine fixed, regroup, and get back offshore and fishing before you know it," I said optimistically.

"Soon?" Stoner held the handrail on the starboard side of the bow, looked down into the water, shook his head, and began to laugh loudly. "We're making great headway. Look, we're keeping right up with the Yoo-hoo box!" He pointed down with a greasy finger. I hesitated, and then followed the direction of Stoner's index finger to see the empty box next to the *Hannah Boden*'s hull, exactly where I had tossed it so very many hours ago. We were drifting, not sailing at all. We would miss the entire month of February at this rate. I should not have been here. This was my trip off. I had to talk some sense into Brownie and convince him that this was silly. He was certainly cutting off his nose to spite his face. I wondered how I could get him to call for a tow. I went over it in my mind, choosing my words carefully. Certainly Bob would be reasonable enough to understand that a missed trip would be financially devastating, and paying for a tow would be relatively inexpensive, and surely the insurance company would cover the cost.

Before I had summoned up enough courage to approach him, Bob came out onto the bow and looked down at the box. He sighed a sad sort of sigh, I thought. He put his hands on his hips and took a deep breath. Then he scolded, "Who threw that box in the water?" I admitted to being the litterbug, stressing the fact that it had been the previous afternoon when I had chucked it overboard. Brownie told me to get a gaff and fish the box out and throw it in the garbage where it belonged. He was mad. I did as I was told and was thoroughly disgusted with myself for littering, being caught littering, and not presenting my rehearsed plea to put an end to this sailing skit. Just as I pulled the punctured box from the gaff hook, Brownie cheerfully announced that we had successfully sailed within low-power VHF range of St. Croix and that a towboat would soon be reaching us. So that was it. My boss didn't want the rest of the fleet to have the satisfaction of hearing him call for a tow on the SSB radio. We would be rescued from an eternity of drifting, and no one would be the wiser. There were a few "Yo-ho-hos" from above, and some heated bitching from below. I kissed the Yoo-hoo box before chucking it into the trash.

As I finished my story, there was sufficient peripheral noise and activity to make me feel as though I could attempt seriousness once more, so I would risk being shot down again. Before I mustered up the courage, Alden spoke up. "Bob Brown. I loved that man. When he went tits up, I thought it was a real loss to the fishing world. What a shame."

"Well, he'd had some warnings . . . high cholesterol, overweight. He was a worker. He pushed himself right into an early grave. Speaking of which, don't you think you've been around long enough to think about end for ending?" I braced myself. I was surprised by the low volume, even-tempered reply.

"Don't you waste another second worrying about me. I'm one tough motherfucker. I'm not ready for end for ending, thank you. In fact, all my parts are bearing an even strain."

BAR SNACK

THE ROYAL TAR

Sea stories, like all types of tales, get a little better, more colorful and detailed, with each telling. Some of the older local stories set around my home have grown to the rural equivalent of "Urban Myths," epic saltwater sagas that become increasingly extreme as they are passed down through many generations of islanders. These stories, unlike the folks who share them, do not age or get decrepit. In fact, quite the opposite is true. My all-time personal favorite is the story of the *Royal Tar.*

Back in 1836, the residents of Deer Isle, Maine, lined the waterfront to see the *Royal Tar* pass through their main thoroughfare on her way to Portland. The *Royal Tar* was a brand-new steamship, built in the Canadian Maritimes and designed to haul freight and passengers between Maine and Nova Scotia. The sighting of any foreign (unusual) vessel was a form of entertainment in this tiny, remote fishing village. This particular day the *Royal Tar* was regarded as quite a spectacle, as it was rumored that she carried onboard an entire traveling circus, complete with animals and a brass band.

As the 160-foot *Royal Tar* majestically passed, someone in the crowd of onlookers noticed smoke rising from an aft compartment on which there was no smokestack. Fire was rightfully suspected. Suspicion became fear as the smoke billowed. The crowd waved and yelled in attempts to alert the captain and crew, but these men had grown so accustomed to drawing attention that they assumed this was an unusually hearty greeting from the islanders, starved for a bit of curiosity. People were now screaming and running along the shore flailing their arms and waving pieces of clothing like signal flags, keeping abreast of the *Royal Tar* as she slowly and proudly made her way west. Circus performers lined her rail, smiling and waving back in appreciation of this enthusiastic crowd of well-wishers.

Some of the local lobster fishermen manned their boats and put chase to the ship that would soon be fully engulfed in flames and too far from shore for her passengers to safely swim. But these small sailing vessels could not begin to catch the big steamship. Finally, someone aboard the *Royal Tar* discovered the fire and pandemonium took over. Because the circus elephant was too large to travel below with the other exotic animals, two of the ship's four lifeboats had been left behind to accommodate the beast on deck. The captain gave the order to release all of the animals from their cages and force them overboard to fend for themselves rather than allow them to burn to death. The elephant freaked out and jumped over the rail directly into one of the lifeboats that had been deployed. This resulted in the death of the animal and the total destruction of the lifeboat.

It was September and the water was cold. The passengers were hesitant to abandon ship, but they knew they would perish if they remained aboard. The water was not only cold, it was now full of wild animals. The bearded lady was the first to take the plunge, and she swam for one of the many tiny islands dotting the area. The lion, tiger, and bears now had the Deer Islanders scrambling toward the safety of their homes, so it's hard to say if there were any witnesses to what transpired beyond this point. All that is known is that the *Royal Tar* burned and sank.

It was weeks before the tide rose high enough to carry the bloated and stinking elephant from the town's shore. For years, people picnicking on the various uninhabited islands claimed sightings of huge snakes, and it is rumored that a local farmer shot and killed the Bengal tiger after it consumed most of his livestock. As a young girl, I heard stories of strange crossbreedings of indigenous and exotics—like the "bear-rabbit" my grandfather warned us of. And, as an adult, I have yet to confirm or discount theories of circus freaks colonizing some of the outer islands of Penobscot Bay.

11

ALL FISHERMEN
ARE LIARS

The night was growing old when Tommy left the bar for a smoke, heading out to the sidewalk with an unlit cigarette dangling from his lower lip, anxious to contaminate the crisp, frosty evening air. I had been on my feet with my coat on for the last two rounds of drinks, but seemed to be having trouble calling it a night. It was ten o'clock, and other than hosting a few stragglers, the Dry Dock was quiet. Waitresses were busy washing tables and sweeping floors, an indication that we, Alden and I, should be shoving off. George was back at our table along with a pair of young fishermen whom I had not met. These guys had come in for a nightcap, having just returned from five days offshore. They recognized Alden, as most fishermen in the area do, and wanted to meet "the legend" and talk salt before climbing back aboard their vessel for a quick nap until 3:00 A.M., when they would "lump out," or off-load their fantastic catch, at the Portland Fish Exchange.

"So, what are you two young fellas going to do when the federal government finally succeeds in putting us out of business?" Alden certainly had a way of putting a damper on the boys' celebratory drink. Alden didn't manage to elicit the fiery responses from the two men that he intended. Instead, they politely informed us that they were both college students fishing through school breaks to fund their educations, and had neither the interest nor the aptitude for life at sea. (Sounded familiar to me, except I fell in love with the sea and called my formal education quits after college.) "Yeah, fishing is not for everyone," Alden remarked. "Some fishermen never figure that out. Most people just aren't cut out for it." Alden stared intently at George, hoping to get a rise out of him.

George, who had been "holding court" as he held down both the end of the bar and one edge of our table, was primed and ready to take Alden on. I had been watching this game from the sidelines for as many years as Alden and I had been friends. Guys, in my opinion, love to berate their best buddies; it's a form of bonding. It's an odd way to display fondness, even affection. Alden, George, and Tommy dug deep into their memories and imaginations to pull out the nastiest insults and degradations they could lay their tongues to, and no one would end up with hurt feelings. In fact, they considered this to be fun.

George's eyes always appear to be at half-staff, the upper lids drooping and veiling the top 50 percent of his eyeballs. When George prepares to launch a barrage, which he did now, he puts his head down, chin to chest, peeks out from under those lazy eyelids, and shakes a pointed index finger at his audience or target. The last time I saw George in this pose was also in a barroom near closing time when he went into some kind of trancelike state. Suddenly from the trance sprang a performance that reminded me of the most exuberant television evangelist. He preached and shook and spoke in tongues and even experimented with a little "faith healing" when he kicked a crutch out from under some poor bastard trying to make it to the men's room. Weirdly, I find George's drunken outbursts as exhilarating as Neil Diamond's "Brother Love's Traveling Salvation Show," which happens to be one of my all-time favorite songs. So I, for one, was ready for the show and was most interested in hearing how George might counter Alden's insinuation that perhaps he and Tommy were ill suited for commercial fishing.

As George stayed himself, getting ready to launch into his performance, Tommy reentered the room accompanied by a gust of cold, smoky air and a large woman I knew only as "Madame Mare." The Madame, ten years ago, had been known as a "coke whore," plying the waterfront bars looking for men willing to barter lines of cocaine for love. Now that cocaine had become passé, the Madame had gained a lot of weight, mostly in her ass, which Alden observed was "two ax handles across," a result of the partaking of massive quantities of alcohol. Although I considered the Madame more a Knickerbocker beer and Doritos type, she ordered a martini, showing that she was keeping up with recent trends. Tommy politely offered Mare the seat that George had vacated; George felt a need to stand and deliver what I suspected would be a stellar performance. The Madame sat and smoothed the outer windblown strands of her hair, stiff with hairspray, back into place over the teased mess beneath. I supposed that in her heyday, Mare would have been described as a tart. But now she was an overweight drunk sporting too much makeup. Still, she was *our* drunk, and we were glad to see her.

Alden, assuming the role of host, greeted the Madame pleasantly and explained that she had just walked in on a discussion of the well-known fact that not everyone was made to go to sea. Mare threw her head back and laughed loudly; this clearly tickled her in some way. When the final chortle rolled from that neck of remarkable girth, Mare daintily wiped a tear from the corner of her eye with an enormous red-polished fingernail. She pulled herself together and spoke of *her* only experience offshore with childish delight. She first defined the time frame as "back in my rowdier days," which I took to mean when she was young and limber enough to do more than waddle to the next bar stool—we were going back at least twenty-five years, as Mare appeared to be pushing sixty years of age.

Mare had sparked a bit of life into our sleepy party, and George waited for her to tell her story of her one experience at sea. There was no way I was going to leave now. So I took my coat back off, found a chair, ordered another glass of wine, and got ready to hear the Madame's tale. It all began on a night not unlike any other. Mare was barhopping with the crew of a longline vessel that was preparing to head to sea for thirty days. The five fishermen with whom she partied drank as much and as quickly as they could, lavishly buying rounds for friends and strangers alike, lest they head offshore with money remaining from the previous trip—taboo. The men, with Mare in tow, had left a wake of destruction the length of Commercial Street, visiting and being tossed from drinking establishments on either side of the busy thoroughfare. By the time they reached the last bar, they had already ripped pay phones from walls, mooned innocent bystanders, peed down through the open sunroofs of parked cars, and engaged in fistfights. No one phoned the police until this last stop, where the men refused to accept the words "last call." They couldn't be shut off! Why, they still had cash!

When the blue lights swirled outside the door, the largest man of the crew decided it was indeed time to leave, and he did so with a rubber-tree plant under one arm and a kicking and screaming waitress under the other. The rest of the crew remained in the bar to ensure that assault-and-battery charges would be filed along with resisting arrest, disturbing the peace, vandalism, and indecent exposure. That night, the police were happy to oblige and decided to arrest all the men—no easy task. Mare sat and quietly sipped her cocktail while glasses, nightsticks, and bodies flew. By the time she had finished her drink, the liquored-up crew was handcuffed and in the paddy wagon. Even the man who fled with tree and waitress was easily apprehended and complained loudly of a burn on his chest where the waitress had crushed out the man's own cigarette.

But now Mare had a problem: The sailors had promised her a room at the posh Eastland Hotel earlier in the evening, and when, through the open window of the police car, she questioned them about the possibility, she was instructed to wait for them aboard the boat, as they would not be detained long. They had some serious hell to raise before embarking on another thirty days of "sea-hab," the backbreaking, sleep-depriving, sobriety-rendering job of longlining swordfish east of the Grand Banks of Newfoundland.

Mare knew well the power of a determined drunk, so she figured they would be true to their word and come and find her. Plus, she had nowhere else to go. Somehow, she staggered to the boat and managed to climb aboard. Mare sat in the galley and chain-smoked, patiently waiting for her new friends to return. She was getting pretty sleepy. Now, Mare did not recall what type of drugs she had washed down with the alcohol that night, nor did she recall passing out at the table, but she clearly remembered coming to at that same galley table two hundred miles from the closest bar, with a captain in command who was not amused. Nor was he willing to turn the vessel around to off-load Mare. The men, whom the captain had bailed out of jail, had already cost him several hours of aggravation. To take the "new cook" ashore, simply because she had changed her mind about the trip, was not in the cards. When she accused her friends of kidnapping her, they easily convinced Mare that this had been her idea, and that they had pleaded with the captain to secure her the site.

"Seasick? I am the worst. I get queasy watching Lloyd Bridges," Mare confessed to us with a smile. "I was flat on my back for the first week. And I'm not talking about sex! That was forbidden by ship's law, along with drugs, alcohol, and fighting. Thirty-two days! I'll never forget it." Mare told us how the crew was so sweet in trying to cure her of seasickness. They tried a variety of remedies, with a constant flow of Saltine crackers and urgings for her to get out on deck for some fresh air. "Fresh? It's been over twenty years, and I can still smell the fish guts and diesel fumes."

After about a week, Mare was able to move gingerly around the deck during the calm days, always clutching the rail or something else substantial to steady herself. "I was pretty much useless, even when I was feeling good, which was not often." Mare could not cook. That was obvious after her first attempt, so she was told not to bother with that duty. She couldn't operate anything hydraulic. She lacked coordination, and the moving parts scared her. She could not bear to *watch* fish being gutted, nor could she stomach the smell of bait. No one trusted her to stand watch, so she just hung on and prayed for the nightmare to end. "I swore off drugs and alcohol that trip, but the second the boat kissed the dock, I figured that any worthy God would have known I had lied. What a way to live . . . I honestly do not know how you guys do it," Mare added, motioning to George and Tommy.

"Jesus! What are you looking at them for?" Alden was getting excited. "They're imposters! They should be working in the shoe store, or pumping gas or something. I'm the fisherman!" Because Mare had stolen George's thunder with her story, George was less riled up now, and sat smiling menacingly at Alden. The two young fishermen took advantage of this lull and excused themselves to hightail it out of the bar. As they turned for the door, the Madame reached out and pinched one of them on the cheek of his ass. When he looked back in astonishment, Mare pursed her lips and blew a kiss, winking in her most seductive manner. In disgust and horror, the boys quickened their already fast pace to the nearest exit. We had all had enough to drink to find this obscenity humorous, and when we stopped laughing, Alden said, "Ah, they're good boys, and smart to be getting educated for something other than fishing. Everyone I know is trying to get out of what's left of this industry. I'm too old to do anything else. How *did* you guys ever happen to get into this racket?" Alden's emphasis on "did" and baffled expression were insulting, I thought. But George and Tommy are not particularly sensitive and now had an opportunity to try to justify their existence. It was a kindness of sorts. George had been itching to tell a story. Now he had a proper invitation. So he did most of the talking while Tommy chimed in occasionally. George began:

"When I was a young man, I will say a young and intellectually naive man, my best buddy, Tommy, and I decided we were going to be world-famous sport-fishing notables, gracing the covers and certainly included in the 'ask the experts' sections of fishing periodicals throughout the world. We should have remembered a fellow named Bradley who wrote for one of the same fishing and boating magazines many years ago. When asked for a definition of good seamanship, his response was 'Never get yourself into a situation where you have to use it.' Well, having spent many years fishing the Chesapeake Bay for rock- and bluefish, we wondered, How hard could it be?"

Now Tommy sat up and added, "We were real men. So why would we ask anyone for advice?"

"We could do this on our own," George continued. "We needed help from no one! We had visions of backing into the dock, marlin flags flying, giving our fans the look of eagles. We were bold and gifted anglers. We knew we would have to move quickly to establish our reputations. So the planning began."

"Wasn't it Frank Lloyd Wright who said, 'God is in the details'?" Tommy asked jokingly.

"Details be damned! We were on a mission to make our fortune. The plan: Once we were famous, lucrative endorsement contracts would be thrown at our feet—and movie deals would follow. It was not quite as difficult as a moon landing, but as we were to find out later, we had underestimated a few things."

"Yeah. Like our stupidity," added Tommy.

"Yes, you are right," said George. "I have always given you more credit than you deserve. I am, as you know, quite generous in that way. Now, to continue. The first item was in choosing a steed on which we would ride to glory. At that time, I owned a twenty-six-foot cruiser and Tommy had a twenty-three-foot center console. These certainly would not do. I sold mine, and Tommy's slab was traded in for a slick thirty-foot sportfisherman, the *Lusty Lady*. Originally, we had intended the boat to be named the *Lucky Lady*. But in our haste to gain the status of God's gift to the angling world, we hired a friend to letter her stern. The unemployed sign painter asked for nothing more than a few drinks in exchange for his time and artistic flair, and in hindsight we realized it would have been wise to compensate him *after* the job was done. So, *Lusty* she was! We were now fully vested in the dream. There was no turning back. God bless us. We were ready to go!

"Since money had become an issue, we decided that our primitive bay rods and reels would have to suffice until we won some tournaments. These were sturdy instruments that had served us well in the past. There was no reason to think that we couldn't overcome the hurdle of inferior equipment. After all, our superior fishing acumen would outweigh all else. We had no use for the newest, most modern, and proven rods and reels. We had the advantage of just being us. Who needed proper tackle?"

"Not us," added Tommy.

"We would also, at least for the first season, have to forgo outriggers and some other equipment of lesser significance."

"Like safety equipment. You know, fire extinguishers, flares. Stuff like that," Tommy explained.

"We would manage. We were enlightened. We were fortunate to procure a slip in Ocean City, Maryland, behind a small hotel, directly across from the most prominent fishing fleet in town. We would have witnesses to our prowess. It just kept getting better. Our dream was becoming a reality!"

"We had arrived," said Tommy.

"That's right, brother! Our budget allowed us a one-week vacation from our daytime jobs. We had the luxury of seven whole days to take our place among the elite: Ernest Hemingway, Zane Grey. The first step in our meteoric rise to the top would be a visit to a tackle shop to acquire lures, charts, bait, and other assorted accessories. We were feeling self-conscious about our lightweight, inshore fishing rods and reels, and concealed them in the boat's cabin so that no one would see them. When we entered the tackle shop, and saw the bright and shiny rigs, we were like kids in a candy store. We did what any red-blooded Americans would do. We pulled out our wallets and maxed out our credit cards to purchase two offshore reels!"

"Praise be to the plastic!" shouted Tommy.

"Hallelujah!" shouted George.

"As luck and the weather gods would have it," George continued, "the forecast for the chosen week was abominable. However, this did not deter us. We decided that we would spend as much time as was humanly possible offshore."

"Ha!" Alden interrupted. "That was your first mistake. You two? Human?"

George chose to ignore Alden. "Our plan was to fish from dawn until midnight if need be, and return to the dock with the catch of a lifetime.

"The first day came. We had plotted and replotted our course. Mind you, this was before the days of loran or GPS." George was pointing the index finger now. "Dead reckoning and a radio-direction finder would guide us to a well-deserved victory. Off we went, just as proud and confident as rookie soldiers."

"The excitement was electric!" Tommy too was now caught up in the reliving of the moment.

"Give me a break," said Alden. Mare hushed him.

"Lines came off reels at five A.M. Destiny was upon us! The wind was blowing from the northeast at twenty knots. We assumed it would drop out a bit as the day progressed. But the wind continued to increase, bit by bit, until we were taking quite a thrashing. The waves were wreaking havoc on our brand-new, untried vessel. I kept my teeth clenched so as not to bite my tongue off, and busily collected the screws and nuts that were vibrating loose and rolling around the deck. The *Lusty Lady* was feeling her oats! After what seemed like days, we finally arrived at Poorman's Canyon—approximately *fifty* nautical miles from shore."

Alden, who couldn't have been more unimpressed, said, "Big deal," before Mare shot him a look and silenced him again.

"Miracle of miracles!" shouted George. "The wind died down to a manageable fifteen knots. We took this as an omen that we were indeed on the fish. This was the spot! It was as clear as a revelation from God above. We turned the boat down sea, put our baits out, and were good to go. We trolled for several hours using our soon-to-be-patented theory of rock-and-roll fishing. It had been expensive installing all eight speakers, but you've got to spend money to make money, right? We played the Rolling Stones, with the base cranked all the way up. Come to think of it, we were ahead of our time in that trend too. Anyway, we blasted the Stones, reasoning that the vibration would drive the fish, like the Pied Piper. You've heard of using dynamite? Well, there's nothing like the Stones to bring the fish up!"

"We did keep a Led Zeppelin tape in reserve in case the Stones weren't cutting it." Tommy seemed to think this an important detail; he somehow felt it made the two of them sound more responsible.

"Atta boy," Alden chimed in. "No safety equipment or a single brain cell between the two of you, but you did have a spare tape handy. Good headwork." At this point I marveled at George's concentration. It appeared that these men could be neither insulted nor embarrassed. George just kept right on talking. And it was quite a sea story, a true epic. In his mind, George was a modern-day Horatio Hornblower, Melville reincarnated, a twin of Tristan Jones, cousin to Patrick O'Brian. And in my mind, he was doing them all justice. I listened intently as George embroidered the rest of his saga, and all the while Alden worked at poking holes in it. By the time the fishing day had wound down, George and Tommy had encountered a tuna seine boat that was no doubt running drugs, a school of ravenous fish that managed to splinter the fishing rods, and a U.S. Navy destroyer in the midst of war games. There was some discussion as to whether the large gray thing that suddenly broke the surface ahead of them had been a whale or a submarine, and nearly an argument about the projectile that narrowly missed their hull. Was it a tuna fish, or a torpedo? Other than on those two points, Tommy corroborated everything—much to Alden's dismay.

Somewhere in the excitement of drag clickers screaming and rods bending dramatically and reels exploding and the weather deteriorating to a full gale, the men managed to land a 200-pound tuna fish. When Alden heard this, he pushed his chair away from the table quickly and yelled, "I don't want to be struck by the lightning bolt intended for you!"

"The adrenaline rush was awesome," George continued. "We had conquered all, and we had done it under tough conditions. There was a lot of high-fiving and back-patting going on. With that two-hundred-pound bad boy dead on our deck, we headed in, anticipating the roar of the crowd and astonished looks from naysayers. The military vessels were still lurking, surveillance, I suppose. I could feel binoculars on my back. I quickly hid the homemade, secret lure that had seduced the tuna. I took my place beside Tommy on the fly bridge, and we started to clear the area.

"It was around nine o'clock and the seas were huge and getting steeper as we crept eastward. It was dark, and the visibility was extremely poor. The *Lusty Lady*'s stern was being pushed to starboard, making it impossible to maintain a good course. She was taking some serious rolls, and when a wave broke over the stern, flooding the cockpit, things got a little tense. The next wave to crash over the stern lifted the port engine hatch and flooded the engine—snuffed it right out. The boat lurched to the right. I thought we would roll over! I had to get the engine restarted pronto. I started down the ladder just as another monstrous sea smashed our stern quarter. We rolled even farther starboard and my feet slipped off the ladder's rung. I was dangling over the starboard side like a sinner over the fiery pit of hell. If I were to drop into this raging sea, I would perish. I thought, How unfair to mankind, to be cheated so. There are miracles!"

"Hey, you forgot the part about the water in the fuel," Tommy suggested helpfully.

"Jesus. One lies, and the other swears to it." At least Alden was smiling now as he realized this tale was coming to an end and he might steal a sliver of the spotlight from George. The waitress had delivered two checks, both of which Alden insisted on paying. We all knew better than to argue, as Alden has some weird phobia about anyone treating him. George did eventually wrap things up, but not until both engines died due to the fuel tank vents not being designed to withstand such severe conditions. I laughed when he admitted to having thrown up all over one engine, and when he bragged of having skillfully repaired both engines using nothing but a Swiss Army knife and the tails of his shirt.

"We obviously limped into safe harbor. But I now know how the crews of the *Monitor* and the *Merrimac* felt during battle. There wasn't much left of the poor fish. When we strung it up at the dock, it looked as though it had come out of a can. When we secured to the dock, Tommy and I looked at each other and both said, 'Maybe we should try commercial fishing.' And here we are," George concluded.

"Well, maybe you should have tried vaudeville. You could bill yourselves as 'The Amazing Bullshit Artists' . . . fishermen, my ass," Alden stammered. "What a couple of clowns! War games, drug runners, and torpedoes all in one day?" Alden was up to his usual. He is always vocal about certain people not belonging on the ocean; he firmly believes he is part of a privileged class in which very few deserve membership: true fishermen.

Before George could come to his own defense, Mare spoke up again. "I've known a lot of fishermen through the years—intimately—and as different as you all are, the one thing you have in common is an inability to tell the truth." Now Mare raised her glass for a toast and proclaimed, "All fishermen are liars." She seemed quite pleased with this statement and waited for the rest of us to clink glasses with her. I hesitated. Why would I drink to that? Especially as she was clearly calling me a liar too, guilty by association—as I am a fisherman.

Finally, Alden raised his coffee cup to Mare's martini glass and repeated, "All fishermen are liars. I'll drink to that." Then he turned and met George square in the eye, and with a devilish grin said, "But not all liars are fishermen."

EPILOGUE

For a period of about two years, I worried that my best friend, Alden Leeman, was on the brink of death. Our long night of the soul at the Dry Dock, chronicled in this book, took place in the middle of this two-year period. During those years, if I phoned him and got no answer, I was convinced that he had collapsed in a heap at the helm of his vessel or had died in his sleep. I wondered how many days would go by before his body would be discovered. I am happy to report that as of this writing, Alden is not only out of the woods, but is doing better than ever. His medications were changed or adjusted, giving him back much of the energy he was lacking in those two scary years of close calls. He works as hard as ever, fishing on days when the weather keeps many men ashore, and has lost over thirty pounds.

In the epilogue of a previous book, *The Lobster Chronicles,* I reported that Alden was then in the process of having a new wooden boat built. As Alden mentioned earlier in this book, he has now taken delivery of her, and she's a beauty! I had at one point postponed plans to build a new boat myself, as I was certain I would inherit Alden's new vessel. Happily, it doesn't appear as though I'll be heir to any of Alden's things in the near future, so I am back to planning. Our friendship has endured, and is sustained mostly with a weekly telephone call and an occasional lunch or dinner. We don't get the opportunity to hang out together often, as Alden simply refuses to travel. He loves Orr's Island, Maine, where he was born and has lived all of his seventy years, and he loves his work, so he has little desire to leave either.

I have heard about people who have had near-death experiences or have cheated death and come out better people for it. You know, the guy who survives a massive heart attack and suddenly stops drinking and swearing. A new lease on life seems in some cases to make the survivor kinder or more considerate, as she or he now has a new appreciation for being on the right side of the dirt. This, I'm glad to report, has not been the case with Alden. He is still the cantankerous old curmudgeon that he's been for all of the twenty-four years we've been friends. He still lectures me relentlessly. He still makes a point of having coffee with the local lobstermen just for the opportunity to refer to them as "puddle fishermen" or "the boys of summer." He relishes spreading discontent and thrives on pissing people off. He is still braggadocious, and in fact has just, in my opinion, discovered a truly odd thing to brag about. Alden's latest boast is that he's a slow eater. Just last week, I stood in Alden's living room, where I was surrounded by trophies and awards and photographs depicting his accomplishments—from a plaque congratulating him on being a

Top Gun fighter-jet pilot to statues for the first, biggest, and most fish caught in the Bailey Island tuna tournament. His home is a veritable shrine to himself. Given all of this, I couldn't believe Alden had resorted to crowing about his "talent" for eating slowly. "I can make a hot dog last all the way from Brunswick to the Gurnett Bridge—driving the speed limit!" He was beaming as he told me this. And it truly is quite a feat. If you believe him.

ACKNOWLEDGMENTS

To a great extent, I attribute any success I've had as a fisherman to my ability to surround myself with good, competent people. The same holds true when it comes to my writing, and I send gracious thanks to those at Hyperion and the Stuart Krichevsky Agency. My editor, Will Schwalbe, is simply the best.

At the risk of leaving someone out, I would like to acknowledge the following people for sharing their tales with me: Archie Jost, David Marks, Brad Kraai, Jeff Waxman, Gus Forbush, George Pusey, Jack Flaherty, Dave Rearick, and Tom Ring. Thanks, guys! I am very appreciative of the many people who told me stories that I did not use, and hope to have an opportunity in the future to put some of these salty tales onto the printed page. Parker Calvert, you are far too much a gentleman to be included in this collection of riffraff and I thank you for your time and story.

A special thanks also to Simon, whose friendship, kitchen, and computer became mine while I was working on this book. You can have your computer back now.